CAR COLLECTOR'S
HANDBOOK

A Comprehensive Guide to Collecting
Rare and Historic Automobiles

by Peter Sessler

HPBooks
a division of
PRICE STERN SLOAN
Los Angeles

Published by HPBooks
a division of Price Stern Sloan, Inc.
11150 Olympic Blvd., Sixth Floor
Los Angeles, California 90064
© 1992 Peter Sessler

10 9 8 7 6 5 4 3 2 1

Library of Congress Cataloging-in-Publication

Sessler, Peter C., 1950-
    Car collector's handbook : a comprehensive guide to collecting
rare and historic automobiles / by Peter Sessler.
        p.   cm.
    Includes index.
    ISBN 1-55788-039-5 : $14.95
    1. Antique and classic cars—Collectors and collecting—Handbooks,
manuals, etc.   I. Title.
TL7.A1S47   1992
629.222´2´075—dc20   91-37220
                                                        CIP

This book is printed on acid-free paper.

Cover photos by Peter Sessler.
Interior photos by Peter Sessler unless otherwise noted.

Acknowledgment

Special thanks to Jim Cox, Vince Lobosco, Paul Mclaughlin and to my wife, Nilda.

Dedication

This book is dedicated to the car collector—through whose toil and effort a small part of our fleeting past has been preserved and continues to be maintained.

About the Author

Peter C. Sessler has had an enduring interest in cars since he was a teenager in the 1960s. Growing up during the musclecar era made a lasting impression on him. As a result he owned, modified and eventually restored several cars, including a 1969 Boss 429 Mustang and 1968 Shelby Mustang convertible. Several of his cars have been featured in national magazines including *Hot Rod Magazine*. Peter Sessler's writing career began in the late 1970s when he contributed articles to club magazines. Eventually these led to a monthly column in *Super Ford Magazine*. Feature articles have since appeared in a number of magazines including *High Performance Pontiac*, *High Performance Mopar*, *Hot Rod's Mustang* and *Vette*. His first book, *Illustrated High Performance Mustang Buyers Guide* was published in 1983. Other books include *Musclecar Greats, Illustrated Jeep Buyers Guide, Camaro/Firebird Performance and Handling Guide* and *The Red Book* series. Peter lives with his wife and four children in Milford, Pennsylvania.

TABLE OF CONTENTS

INTRODUCTION

Nostalgia is one of the fundamental factors that propels the car collector hobby. Many people can now afford the cars they dreamed about when they were younger, and purchase these cars to help them stroll down memory lane.

The hobby of collecting and restoring vintage automobiles began before the second World War, when lovers of old cars banded together to form organizations to preserve Brass Era vehicles (Pierce-Arrow, Model T Ford, etc.) built from the turn of the century through the Twenties.

As generations passed, the classics of the Thirties and early Forties (Duesenburgs, Packards and Cadillacs, for example) became popular as collectors of Brass Era cars retired or became too elderly to continue with their hobby. For the baby boom generation born after WW II, the cars of the Fifties and Sixties grew in popularity and eventually replaced the Classics and the Model A Ford as popular collectible automobiles.

Regardless of the generation or era, the focus of what makes a car collectible has never changed, although that definition has slowly evolved in the past few years as the old car hobby grew and more people became involved.

Why People Collect Cars

Fundamentally, two factors propelled the growth of the old car hobby—nostalgia and investment. The impact that the automobile had on Twentieth Century America is virtually impossible to measure. It changed our lifestyles and became part of our culture. We grew up with cars, and the part they played in our early lives creates fond memories. This nostalgia for the past centers around the automobile, and for generations of collectors, reaching back across the decades and reviving a tangible piece of one's past is the cornerstone of the old car hobby.

Gather old car enthusiasts together to reminisce and they'll start remembering a specific song on the radio of a specific car at a specific time. Some measure the times of their lives by particular cars they drove. They'll remember the excitement of each September when the new cars were introduced, about TV commercials and magazine ads that depicted a flash of chrome or the edge

Ground-pounding musclecars, such as a 454 Chevelle, have become highly prized by collectors and enthusiasts during recent years. The most valuable Chevelle is one equipped with the rare LS6 454 engine.

of a gleaming fender tantalizingly exposed by the edge of a lifted cover. From 1946 to the late Sixties, America flocked to dealerships to peer through whitewashed showroom windows for a glimpse of the new cars, and on introduction day crowds filled the showrooms to look, touch, sit in and marvel at Detroit's "all new" offerings.

Times have changed, and new cars today tend to look like last year's models. We fondly look back on "the good old days" and the cars whose brochures we collected and filled our dreams. That's part of what makes a car collectible.

For others, emotional meaning takes a back seat to investment, and for these collectors, rarity and specialty are what defines a car as collectible. Can a car whose production totals in the millions, such as the Ford Mustang for example, have any collector value? The answer is yes, because although millions of Mustangs were built, there are a few Mustang models that were produced in relatively small numbers, most notably the per-

formance models such as the Boss 302 and 429. These have true collector value because they are unique and some may have automotive historical significance. For example, Ford built 1,628 street Boss 302 Mustangs in 1969 so that the car would be allowed to race in the SCCA Trans-Am race series. Another example would be the 1965-1969 Shelby Mustangs.

Other cars may stand out because they were equipped with a fairly unusual option or option combination. For example, a Mustang that came with a front bench seat stands out because 99% of all Mustangs came with bucket seats. But is it a true collectible? Someone trying to sell it to you would have you believe so. A true collectible must not only be produced in relatively low numbers, but it must also be unique (limited production engines or special historical significance are valid credentials). For example, the 602 1967 Z28 Camaros built were the first of a long line of Z28s, and they were also the first American musclecars that stressed balance as one of its

Can a car like the Mustang, with production in the millions, be considered a true collectible? The answer is yes, especially rare models with limited option availability. Convertibles like this '65 are also considered more valuable than garden variety hardtops because they were produced in lower numbers, and are more desirable.

Ford built very limited numbers of Boss 429's in 1969 and 1970 only to homologate the 429 engine for NASCAR Winston Cup racing. Therefore, they are prized by collectors. Photo by Michael Lutfy.

Race cars, such as this Trans-Am Boss 302 once raced by George Follmer, have high collector value and appeal, and are often raced at vintage car events. This is the car at speed in the 1991 Palm Springs Vintage Grand Prix. Photo by Michael Lutfy.

performance parameters—good handling, braking and acceleration without the use of a big-block V-8. For that reason, they stand above many other Camaros of that era. That doesn't mean that the 1963 six-cylinder Chevy Impala you learned to drive on isn't an interesting car, because it is. And to some hobbyists it's a collectible. But it isn't in the same league as a 409 1963 Super Sport Impala convertible, which has far more desirability as a collectible to considerably more people.

THE COLLECTIBLE CAR AS AN INVESTMENT

The modern era of car collecting began in the late Seventies as baby boomers, now affluent enough to purchase the cars of their youth, snapped up late Fifties cars and musclecars of the Sixties.

As more people poured into the hobby, a service indus-try grew to serve the restorer and collector. Dozens of magazines were launched and hundreds of books were written about marque histories and restoration techniques. Restoration shops appeared to rebuild and restore these cars, and hundreds of reproduction parts businesses flour-ished. Because these cars were becoming more popular, their value climbed through the decade of the Eighties. Average appreciation was between 10 and 20 percent per year. Hobbyists could justify the money that went into a restoration because they would break even once the car was completed and could look forward to their car build-ing a little equity in the future. And, unlike stocks or mutual funds, these investments could be enjoyed and driven occasionally.

That changed to a great degree when the stock market took a tumble in 1987. Many investors were scared out of the stock market, and some of them took to collecting tangibles—art, precious stones and for some, vintage

The significant history of the LeMans-winning Ford GT-40s add to their tremendous value. The skyrocketing prices of cars like this GT-40 and many Ferraris during the 80's sent collector car prices ballistic.

automobiles. By 1989, collector cars were considered as safe an investment as real estate, and the cream of the collector crop—Ferraris particularly—went ballistic. Soon they were too expensive for all but the very rich, and investors turned to Corvettes and musclecars like Hemi Mopars, big-block Chevrolets and Shelbys.

As the values of these skyrocketed, prices for more mundane musclecars also rose, which was great for those already firmly entrenched in the hobby but tough for those who wanted to participate but lacked large financial resources. Suddenly, musclecars were the darling of the investment set, many of which didn't know a tie rod from a tow bar.

Advantages & Disadvantages

All of this heady activity finally came to a crash in 1990, and values on certain cars that had been overpriced tumbled back to what hobbyists believed were more realistic figures. Hemi 'Cudas, for example, that had changed hands for as much as $175,000 were now selling for half

that, and 1967 427cid/435hp Corvettes that had commanded $125,000 were, by 1991, begging at $50,000. Many lost money on these cars, and by 1991, investors had left the playing field, leaving the remains to the hobbyists, who felt they had regained control of their hobby.

Today, buying a collectible car with an eye toward investment must be jaundiced. While prices have fallen to more realistic levels, the general consensus is they will rise again, however not to the inflated levels of the late Eighties. Buyers today must be willing to accept appreciation levels of 5 to 15 percent annually. Like real estate, which also dropped in the early Nineties, buying a collectible for investment purposes today is speculative. One thing is for sure, with lower prices now prevailing, more traditional hobbyists are returning to the fold and for the most part, the old car hobby has shaken out the wild prices paid for models just a few years earlier.

Whether your motivation to enter the old car hobby is powered by nostalgia or investment, owning a collectible car (restored or not) can be an enjoyable experience. Like

5

Early Porsches, like the 356 models, are popular with collectors, but race cars like this '66 906 are extremely rare and priced beyond the reach of most people. Again, Porsche's racing history adds value to their previous race cars. In order for a race car to have maximum value, it must be documented. Photo by Michael Lutfy.

the tens of thousands of people before you who have been involved with collectible cars, you'll find that there are some fundamentals to the hobby that can make your ownership of an old car a pleasant experience. Consider this book a manual to guide you through the maze of entering the hobby, choosing the right vehicle and then learning the fun of restoring, maintaining and showing your collectible car.

—Paul Zazarine
Editor, *Corvette Fever*

WHAT MAKES A CAR COLLECTIBLE?

While it's true that collectivity is in the eye of the beholder, the consensus within the old car hobby is that certain rules of thumb prevail in determining what is considered an investment grade collectible.

- Because of their usually lower production numbers and popularity, convertibles are generally worth more than hardtop models.

- Special editions with particular body work or interior upholstery.

- Manufacturer's show or pace cars (must be documented).

- High performance models with the most potent engine and drivetrain options; especially low production models like the 1971 Hemi 'Cuda convertible (seven built).

- First year production of a special model (1955 Chrysler 300 or 1964 GTO are good examples).

- Race cars (must be documented)

There has been significant growth in the popularity of musclecars built during the Sixties and early Seventies. Chevy's 454 engine, which debuted in 1970, was the epitome of American power. It also marked the beginning of the end of the musclecar movement, which would all but cease by the end of 1973.

During the height of the car collector boom, '67 427 Corvettes were selling for as much as $125,000. However, current price values have fallen off to the $50,000 range. Photo by Michael Lutfy.

The frenzied car collecting activity during the Eighties led to wild speculation. Many people invested heavily in limited production cars, such as this Corvette ZR-1, by paying thousands more than the sticker price. These same people also lost money in 1990 as the car collector market crashed and leveled out. However, as the ZR-1 was produced in very low numbers, it may still prove to be an extremely valuable collector car in the years to come. Photo by Michael Lutfy.

WHAT TO BUY & WHERE TO FIND IT

The desirability and value of a 1954 Corvette is only surpassed by its predecessor, the 1953. Finding one in good condition, that is authentic and documented, may require careful research that goes beyond perusing the newspaper classifieds.

Unless you enter the market with a specific car in mind, you may make the wrong purchase. Deciding which car to buy will depend on a number of factors. Do you favor one car maker over another? Are you looking for a pony car, musclecar or luxury car? Do you want a convertible or hardtop? How about options and accessories? Is this car being purchased solely for fun or do you want to turn a profit? Finally, your financial resources will be a determining factor. Perhaps you want an LS6 SS454 Chevelle, but your financial grasp can only reach as far as the less expensive SS396 model. Be willing to accept what you can afford—it's possible you'll be able to move up to the LS6 in the future.

RESEARCH

Research is the first step in deciding which car to buy. Not only must you be aware of the different models, body colors, options and accessories that were offered, you must be knowledgeable about the proper engines and codes specific to the car you choose. Fortunately, there are a multitude of books offered on the subject, almost all of them available from Classic Motorbooks (P.O. Box 2, Osceola, WI 54020 (800-826-6600). Motorbooks has a large, comprehensive catalog (free) that is full of titles on marque histories, buyer's guides and other reference material. These books will provide solid information on which models are more desirable and why, along with other valuable information such as production figures, clubs and part sources.

Hemmings Motor News

To put your finger right on the pulse of the old car hobby, the ultimate reference source is *Hemmings Motor News* (P.O. Box 380, Bennington, VT 05201). If you are at all serious about collector cars, then you'll find

9

Hemmings to be an indispensable tool. It contains approximately 800-900 pages of want ads each month in addition to auction and event listings, services offered, books and literature and much more. The only problem with *Hemmings* is that it isn't easy to find. Some newsstands carry it as well as some of the bookstore chains, but most copies are sold through subscription. You can write for more information to the address listed above. Not only will *Hemmings* provide information on where to buy reference material to learn about your favorite collector car, you can also track prices to see if you can afford that LS6 Chevelle. Other good sources for reference include *Cars and Parts* and *Old Cars Weekly* (Krause Publications, 700 E. State Street, Iola, WI 54990).

Clubs—Once you have zeroed in on a specific car and have learned as much as you can about it, join the marque club that supports that particular make or model. Once again, Hemmings will be your source, as most clubs advertise for new members each month. There is also a detailed club list in the appendix. A club will provide you with a monthly newsletter, technical assistance and information about the car you plan to purchase. More on that in a moment.

Hemmings Motor News will be your most valuable resource. A typical issue is about the size of a large metropolitan phone book, and it has a great deal of information about car collecting. To get a copy, contact: Hemmings Motor News, P.O. Box 380, Bennington, VT 05201.

Your choice may be limited by your budget. An LS6 SS454 Chevelle may be your dream, but the price for one may be out of reach. Be prepared to lower your standards; the SS396 Chevelle is more common and therefore more affordable, so you may have to settle for one of those instead. Photo courtesy Musclecar Review.

Most any car that is dubbed as an "Official Pace Car" of the Indianapolis 500 generally has collector value. To commemorate the occasion, the manufacturer will usually offer a "Pace Car" edition of the model with high performance and accessory items not available on the general model, and keep the numbers limited.

WHERE TO FIND YOUR COLLECTOR CAR

After you have decided on which car to buy, you have to know where to look for it. Your starting point should be your local newsstand. There, you'll find a vast selection of car magazines, regional trader-type publications and the local newspaper. You can discount the general interest magazines such as *Motor Trend*, *Road & Track* and *Car and Driver*, which deal primarily with new cars, or the many hot rod type magazines which cover specific automotive areas such as drag racing, stock car racing or the many off-road, trucking and rodding magazines. Look for the collector-type magazines such as *Collectible Automobile*, *Classic Auto Restorer* and magazines that cover a single marque. For example, *Corvette Fever* magazine, as the name implies, focuses on the Chevrolet Corvette, and contains many articles and feature cars relating to restoration. Some of the marque magazines are bi-monthlies so you should make several visits to your newsstand.

Once again, *Hemmings* will be a valuable resource, as there are literally thousands of "cars for sale" classified ads. You need to get a feel for the market to see what others are asking for their cars. Remember that the prices printed in the classified ads are asking prices. Most sell-

11

ers can be negotiated down unless the ad states "firm." Even then, it can't hurt to try with a lower offer.

Classified Ads

Everyone has looked at classified ads at one time or another. You'll find ads that don't tell you much, save for the year and model of the car and a phone number. Other times you'll run into ads that are extremely detailed, listing every option and at the same time recording in meticulous detail what has been done to the car. When it comes to classified ads, it is important to understand what the ads say, and by the same token, what they *don't* say. Read each ad with a jaundiced eye, and don't always believe everything you read. For details on deciphering classified ads, see the sidebars below and on p. 15 and 16.

To get an idea of how condition and options can be described, let's examine both good and bad examples of ads taken from an issue of *Hemmings Motor News*. The phone numbers have been changed, however the cars and their descriptions are verbatim:

CORVETTE: 1963 split window, 327/300, 4-speed, Sebring Silver, all dates and numbers correct, original title and dealer's invoice, excellent all original condition, few cars found like this one. $35,000. PH 203-000-0000.

This ad gives you the basics—a 1963 split-window coupe powered by a 300 hp 327 cubic-inch engine with a four-speed manual transmission. The ad could have included a few more options, mileage and the interior

---

GLOSSARY OF TERMS

After you read a few ads, you'll see that certain phrases and terminology keep cropping up. Listed below are some of the more widely used terms and what they mean:

RESTORED. When you see "restored," it is a sign that you need to ask more questions when you call—such as when was the restoration completed, what was done, who did it, and what condition the car is in now. Sometimes you'll see "ground-up" restoration. This should mean that the car was totally disassembled and put together again with new or refurbished parts. Sometimes you'll see 80% or some other percentage restored. This means that the car is only partially restored. Ask for details about what was and wasn't restored and why.

ORIGINAL. Again, as with "restored" you have to ask "How original is the car?" Is it 100% original? An original car is one that has the original drivetrain, body, and interior.

CORRECT OR FACTORY CORRECT. This means that the car has "correct" parts but it is also another way of saying that the car is not original. The engine, for example, may have been replaced with a factory replacement or service engine of the same size.

NUMBERS MATCH. You'll may run into this phrase. It means that the car is equipped with the original engine, transmission and other parts because they have codes that "match" the date the car was manufactured. For example, the engine block will be coded with for application as well as date of manufacture, as will the heads, intake and exhaust manifolds, alternator, carburetor, etc. Because a "numbers match" car has considerably more value (and a higher price) make sure you verify the numbers and ask to see all documentation.

BEST OFFER. You can interpret best offer ads in three ways. It could be that the seller is asking so much for the car that he is afraid he'll scare away any potential caller, or he simply doesn't know what the car is worth. If you answer such an ad, ask the seller what he is looking to get or at the very least, he should give you a "rough" idea of what he wants for the car. It can also mean that the car is in such poor condition that the seller just wants to get the most he can for it.

Perhaps the best place to find a Cobra is at an auction or in club newsletters like the Shelby American. Once originally priced at about $7000, Cobra's like this 427 sell for hundreds of thousands of dollars. The "CSX 3105" on the front of the car is the VIN number.

color, but rather, the owner choose to stress its originality and documentation. Let's look at another example:

MUSTANG:1964-1/2 conv., white car, red int. great shape, $12,000. PH 404-000-0000.

This is a poor ad. It just doesn't tell you enough. What engine does the car have? What transmission? What options? What constitutes "great shape?" Without more information, you may not want to risk a long distance phone call without checking other ads first. This ad will not generate the number of calls the seller expects. If you respond to an ad of this type, be prepared to ask plenty of questions. For more details, see chapter 2.

Newspapers

Don't discount your local newspaper as a source for finding a collectible car. Many papers have a collectible, antique or specialty section and, since these cars are in your area, you should look there first. That doesn't mean you should overlook the section where current used cars are listed; you may find a 1969 Camaro listed with all the late-model Chevrolets simply because the owner didn't know of the other sections or isn't aware that a 1969 Camaro is considered collectible. Perhaps the paper made a mistake and misplaced the ad. Many local papers have special rates for short-term classified advertising, so you may find the same ad appearing for a week or ten days. Your best bet is to start with the Sunday paper because you'll find the greatest number of ads.

If you live near a large metropolitan area you may also want to consider getting that paper's Sunday edition as well. For example, *The New York Times* is available nationally. You wouldn't think that this would be of any use to someone in Kansas, but you'd be surprised how many out-of-town ads appear in a large metropolitan area paper. Big city papers, such as those found in Los

The owner of a Boss 429 is more likely to advertise his car in an enthusiast magazine like Mustang Monthly or Mustang Illustrated than in the local newspaper. Photo by Michael Lutfy.

Angeles, Chicago, San Francisco, Dallas, Miami and Phoenix are all good sources for ads.

Because the seller placed the ad in a newspaper, there's the possibility he may be more motivated to sell the car. A seller can call the paper on Thursday and know that his ad will appear on the following Sunday. You'll see more "must sell" ads because sellers advertising in newspapers are more anxious to dispose of a car. Advertising in one of the many collector magazines requires a lot of patience because of the long lead times required. This doesn't mean that the seller isn't as anxious to sell; it could be that he's willing to hold the car until the ad breaks in a publication like *Hemmings* because it reaches more potential buyers than newspapers.

Local Car Trader Magazines

After newspapers, these publications are a good source of collectibles for sale in your area. In many cases,

Many national clubs have local chapters throughout the country, and they put on smaller "cruise ins" and "show n' shine" events throughout the year. Your best bet is to go to the show, and talk to the members about the car you want. The members are usually extremely knowledgeable and only too willing to help a fellow enthusiast. They also generally have a good idea as to what cars are for sale in your area. Photo by Michael Lutfy.

The larger national clubs generally publish a newsletter. Some are monthly, others are quarterly. For marque specific, rare cars, it's a good idea to join these clubs and subscribe to the newsletter. Or, in some cases, you can contact the club and just purchase the newsletter before joining. Publications like the Shelby American insist that their members list the VIN numbers along with the ad to verify the authenticity of the car, so you can be assured you're getting what you pay for. Another tip is to place a "car wanted" ad in these newsletters.

photographs accompany the ad. These publications often carry ads for late-model and lower priced cars, along with modified and parts cars. In some markets, the *Auto Trader* issues an *Antique and Collector Car* edition, which will feature ads specifically for vintage collectibles. Again, you'll find that sellers who advertise in these publications are usually willing to settle for a lower price than advertised in order to sell the car quickly.

Enthusiast Magazines

The enthusiast magazines are a good source of information but they may not always be the best source for ads. As stated earlier, some enthusiast "niche" magazines are bi-monthlies, so you may find that by the time the issue is out, the car has been already sold. Even monthly magazines may have a two- or three-

---

RATING COLLECTIBLE CARS BY CONDITION

You'll find that in many ads, the condition of the car is sometimes referred to by its condition. The ratings shown here are the commonly accepted classification system used for collectible cars.

EXCELLENT. This describes a car that has been restored to concours condition. Such a car would be as perfect as it could possibly be with the use of all original components showing original part numbers. This category also includes an original, unrestored car in fantastic condition showing no wear. Such a claim by the seller should be backed with accurate documentation. If the seller doesn't have it, beware.

FINE. A superior restoration, an excellent original that is showing some wear, or a combination of the two.

VERY GOOD. Good original condition, or an older restoration that is showing some age. It also includes an amateur restoration or a restoration that hasn't been done to professional standards.

GOOD. A car that is complete and in running condition but needs restoration. Although they aren't ready for the junkyard, these cars show their age.

RESTORABLE. This category includes cars that need total restoration and may not be in running condition. Though the purchase price may be low, figure on thousands of dollars and hundreds of hours to get it back to shape. This type of car may not be worth considering unless it is very rare or valuable or can be used as a parts car.

---

month lead time. Any seller who advertises in these magazines obviously has more patience and is probably asking more for his car.

On the other hand, you may be able to find a rare model advertised. A seller of a 1969 Boss 429 Mustang is more

RATING COLLECTIBLE CARS BY INVESTMENT POTENTIAL

Besides condition, you may want to refer to an investment rating. One popular rating system is the one used in Motorbooks International's *Illustrated Buyers Guide* series. In addition to their condition, cars are rated by their investment potential with a five star system:

5 STARS. Five stars are used for the rarest and most sought-after cars. These special cars appreciate at a faster rate and hold their value even during a downturn in the market.

4 STARS. Still rare and desirable, these cars are an excellent investment but are somewhat more numerous.

3 STARS. A good entry-level car that may have some future potential depending on color, options and production. They are far more numerous than four-star cars.

2 STARS. Not particularly special, these are common cars that won't appreciate at a fast rate, if at all. Their value depends more on nostalgic appeal.

1 STAR. These cars have little collector appeal or potential. Highly modified, customized cars, "basket cases" and cars with an incorrect drivetrain are in this category.

Specialty car dealers are another route to take, but be forewarned that prices will usually be high. Furthermore, because the cars are sometimes taken on consignment, the salesperson may not know the car's entire history and authenticity, nor have the details on what was restored, replaced, etc. On the other hand, the car you really want just may not be available anywhere else.

likely to advertise his car in *Mustang Monthly* magazine than in the local newspaper. Even though asking prices may be higher, you'll find a higher quality car in enthusiast magazines in most cases.

Clubs

No matter what car you are interested in, there is bound to be a club for it. Just check the appendix at the back of this book. It seems only natural that people want to get together with other people who share the same interests. If you are interested in a Pontiac GTO, you'll stand a good chance of finding one in the *GTO Association of America's* newsletter. You may even want to consider placing a "car wanted" ad. You'll get calls.

Club members are usually very knowledgeable and even if you don't know that much about the car you are interested in, a few well-worded questions will increase your knowledge. In many clubs there are no limitations

Thinking about buying a GTO? How about a Mopar? At this show you've got both lined up beside each other (the Mopars are behind the Pontiacs), with owners only too willing to tell you everything you want to know, like how much their restoration cost, etc. General car shows offer variety, which is helpful if you haven't made up your mind yet. No matter where you live, there's bound to be a large car show open to all makes and models in your area.

on the number of words used in the ad, so just by reading the ads themselves you'll learn a lot about what the owner has done to the car and if the car has a particular history. People who join clubs, then advertise their cars for sale in the newsletters, often know quite a bit about the car and are likely to have all documented information. The car, if in good condition, is likely to have been well taken care of because the owner is a serious enthusiast with a deep appreciation for the car. The problem with club newsletters is a long lead time is required before your membership (if joining the club is a prerequisite) is processed and your first issue arrives. It all depends on how anxious you are to make a purchase. If you are not interested in joining the club, ask the membership secretary if you could buy the current issue (and several past issues) in order to decide what the club is like.

There is also another benefit of club newsletters to consider. Some clubs, for example *The Shelby American Automobile Club*, now require that anyone advertising a Shelby or Cobra must also include the car's VIN in the ad. The club established this policy for two reasons. First, this ensures that only authentic cars are advertised, and second, it enables the club to keep track of the cars whenever they exchange hands. For example, in a recent Shelby Club bulletin it was reported that a 1967 Shelby was advertised in *The New York Times* listing the letter "C" in the VIN. As no Shelbys were built with the 289 cubic-inch two-barrel engine (letter code "C"), the club urged extreme care and caution to any interested parties. This is just one of the advantages of joining a marque club.

Specialty Car Dealers

Many specialty car dealers have sprung up over the past few years. Such dealers may specialize in a particular make or a particular type of collectible. This is an easy way to find the car you are looking for. Most of these dealers advertise in *Hemmings* while others advertise in the local *Auto Trader* and enthusiast magazines.

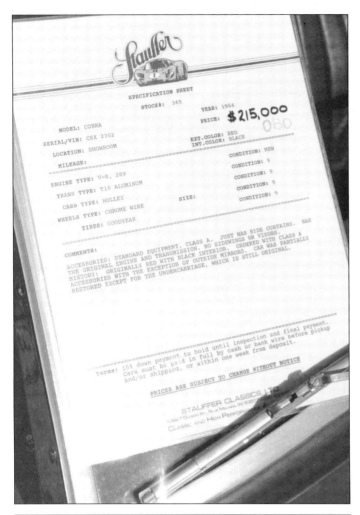

Cars advertised for sale at car shows may have flyers like the ones shown here. As you can see, the one by Stauffer Classics (top) details everything about the Cobra on the sheet, including engine components, condition, price, options and terms for purchase. The GT40 sheet just lists the history and mechanical condition, requiring further inquiry. Photos by Michael Lutfy.

Disadvantages—There are some disadvantages to buying from a specialty dealer. Since the dealer has to make a profit, many of these cars are overpriced. At times, you'll find that the cars they have for sale are on consignment. If the car has been sitting in the showroom for a long time, it may be that the owner has an unrealistic idea of what his car is worth.

A dealer will also be less likely to know of the car's history and possibly its authenticity. It is also possible that the dealer may not know much about the marque, other than the car he has in his showroom is "hot" and that you'd better put a deposit on it right away.

However, there are knowledgeable dealers who are reputable and have been around for a long time and provide good service. It takes research to determine which dealers are reputable and which ones should be avoided. One way to make this determination is to check with the *Better Business Bureau*. Another is to ask fellow club members who may be familiar with a specific dealer's reputation.

Car Shows

Most car shows are held during the spring through early fall months. No matter which part of the country you live in, you're bound to have a show or two occur in your area. Check *Hemmings* or *Old Cars Weekly* for a listing of events. Attending shows can be very beneficial. For one thing, you're bound to see cars similar to the one you are interested in. Talking to their owners, you can find out about the cars and common problem areas. For example, Boss 302 Mustangs are known for their poor quality pistons. This is particularly useful if you are planning to buy an unrestored car. Owners who have been through a restoration will be able to tell you how much it cost and how much time the restoration took to complete. Quite likely you'll see cars for sale too. Often you'll find that club representatives are there which can facilitate the process of joining or just purchasing current and past newsletters.

You'll also find part and literature vendors at the larger shows. If you are fairly new to the hobby, this can increase and broaden your knowledge of the particular make you're interested in. It also provides you with the opportunity to examine restored cars on display and cars that are for sale.

Car shows are great places to buy and sell cars. As a buyer, you get the chance to inspect the car closely, although you may not get the chance to test drive it at the show. However, you can arrange for that later. Photo by Michael Lutfy.

Automotive Flea Markets

Several times a year, usually in the spring and fall, thousands of parts vendors get together for several days at Hershey and Carlisle, Pennsylvania. These two events are quite incredible simply because of the sheer number of vendors that participate (over 8,000) and the tens of thousands of buyers that come looking for cars, parts, literature and memorabilia. With so many sellers, the likelihood of finding that rare part and being able to inspect it in person (rather than over the phone) makes attending such a meet worthwhile. Not only will you be able to find parts, literature and the like, you'll also see lots of cars for sale.

Carlisle-This is the grandaddy of all automotive flea markets, the largest in the United States. It is not uncommon to see 2,000 cars for sale at the Spring or Fall Carlisle events. These events usually start on a Thursday and end on Sunday, and it's not unusual to see signs on cars saying they must be sold by Sunday.

You may think that finding a bargain at Carlisle is impossible; after all, these are all car guys who have been selling parts and cars for years. Interestingly, there are bargains to be found and if you are looking for a car, Carlisle may be the place for you. In fact the organizers of the event have made it as easy as possible to buy a car there. They have a tag and title agency on the premises that can issue temporary plates, if needed. One note of caution: the cars on sale at events like Carlisle may not be correctly restored. But, if you've done your research and learned as much about the car of your choice as possible, the chances of being burned are greatly reduced. If you live in the Northeast or even in other parts of the country, your automotive education isn't complete until you have been to Carlisle or Hershey. If you can't travel that far, there are other major swap meets around the

Automotive flea markets offer some of the best opportunities to inspect and purchase cars and parts. The Carlisle, Pennsylvania swap meet, held in the Spring and Fall each year, is the largest one in the country. It is not uncommon to see over 2000 cars for sale, and up to 8000 vendors selling parts. The promoters even have a title bureau on hand to make your purchase easier. If you're serious about car collecting, don't miss this event.

country that may not be as large as Carlisle, but are still filled with the cars, parts, literature and memorabilia you're looking for.

Auctions

The number of automobile auctions has grown with the collector car market in recent years. Companies like Kruse International and Cole-Yacoobian have established reputations for putting on collector car auctions that have become a barometer for the value of collector cars and the state of the market.

Types—There are two types of collector car auctions— *Consignment* and *Private Owner* auctions. The most common is the Consignment auction. Here, individual car owners consign their cars to the company to sell at the auction. Auction companies are free to accept for consignment whatever type of car they want to. For example, a particular auction may feature only prewar cars, and

that event will draw buyers interested in cars of that era only, making it highly unlikely that the auction company would accept a 1966 SS396 Chevelle for that particular event. Unless specifically stated, most consignment auctions are open to all types of collector cars and trucks.

A private owner auction is usually the result of an estate sale or by a single collector seeking to dispose of his collection. Parts and unrestored cars may also be part of this type of auction.

There is another type of auction, although it doesn't fit within the category of collector cars. Often times, there are local pubic auctions designed to sell cars that have been seized or impounded by police because they were used in the commission of a crime or seized by the IRS. Also, cars that were repossessed or are being disposed of by a company for some reason or another are included in these types of public auctions. Sometimes, cars are sold as part of an estate sale. Although the

Car auctions are another venue where you might find your car at a good price. However, buying at a car auction requires planning and knowledge of the process. The main thing is to be prepared, both financially and with your decision, before attending. Auctions are covered in more detail in chapter 2.

chances are slim, you may happen upon a rare collectible car and end up with a real bargain, because these types of auctions generally do not attract serious investors and/or collectors. These auctions are usually advertised in your local newspaper.

There are a variety of collector car auction companies which hold auctions at various locations throughout the country. Some may only have one or two auctions; others, such as Kruse International hold as many as 40 a year. Some may be held during one or two days; others, such as Kruse's Auburn, Indiana auction (which is billed as the largest of its kind) lasts 6 days and attracts thousands of cars, bidders and spectators.

Although buying a car at an auction is not difficult, you need to understand how they work or you could end up making a serious mistake. For complete details on how to buy your car at an auction (and sell one, for that matter) see chapter 2.

Other Sources

You never know when you'll find the car you've been looking for. Take a Sunday drive in the country and look for "For Sale" signs, especially on the back roads. It's unlikely that you'll uncover a 1953 Corvette this way, but it is possible to find an interesting, probably unrestored collectible. Some people just don't know what they have. Perhaps a car has been sitting in a barn collecting dust and the owner is finally ready to part with it.

New Car Dealer—An unlikely source might be your local new car dealer. Depending on what state you live in, car dealers may or may not be open on Sunday. Assuming they are closed, walk their lot when no one is there. There may be a section of "junkers" or project cars that mechanics are working on. Also, a lot of dealerships changed hands during the Eighties and often they inherited older cars that they had no interest in. I once happened upon a Chevy dealer that had a 1957 supercharged

We've all heard the story about the guy who found a rare car just sitting in a barn collecting dust. . . well, you know the rest. Truth is, finds like that are increasingly rare these days, but you never know. Take a drive in the country and look for "For Sale" signs and autos languishing in backyards. It might behoove you to check out all leads, even if they sound too good to be true. There are still people who don't know the value of what they have. This is a '65 Thunderbird convertible that had been sitting in a barn for years, obviously uncared for by the owner. As they say, "One man's junk is another man's treasure."

Your local new car dealer may have what you're looking for, although it's a long shot. These Chrysler Imperials and '66 Lincoln convertible have been sitting for a few years behind a Chevrolet dealership.

Many new car dealers changed hands during the Eighties, and some dealers inherited old cars they have no interest in. In this case, a Ford dealer inherited this '57 supercharged Studebaker Hawk, yet he hadn't done a thing with it since 1981. This is a perfect example of the moral, "Sometimes you'll find what you're looking for in the most unlikely place."

Studebaker sitting in one of his storage sheds. It had been sitting there for a decade, because the dealer couldn't be bothered to straighten out a minor title problem. Dealers in this situation may not have the time or resources to complete a restoration and may respond to a low offer. You'll never know if you don't ask.

Locator Services—During the Eighties, as the collector car hobby sizzled, locator services sprang up. These companies would, for a fee, locate the car you were looking for. As the collector car market slowed down in the Nineties, there wasn't as much demand for their services and few locator companies remain in operation today.

BUYING YOUR CAR

2

Now that you've decided on which car to buy, and found it, it's time to consummate the deal.

At this point in your quest for a collector car, you should have a solid idea of the kind of car you want, have researched as much as possible about that make and model, and have determined all the available sources where you can make the purchase. The next hurdle is to locate and buy the car. The steps you take now are the most critical in the process. It is essential that you know what to look for and know what questions to ask. Otherwise, you may purchase the wrong car in the wrong condition, souring your entrance into the hobby and costing you money. Even if you consider yourself knowledgeable and have bought dozens of late-model cars, buying a vintage car requires far more care and scrutiny. Even veterans of car collecting have been burned on occasion.

Let's assume you've made a choice about the make and model you want—let's say a 1965 Mustang GT convertible—and you've researched all you can about the car.

Is it wise to "settle" for an equally nice regular Mustang convertible that you've located or to keep looking? Sometimes it can be exasperating trying to find the right car; there are many "nice" cars available. Knowing exactly what you want and sticking to that choice can be difficult. Just remember that if you lower your sights and purchase the first "nice" car you see, you may regret it later on. You may have to pass up plenty of "nice" cars along the way. Stick to your game plan and get the car you really want.

With so many different methods of buying a collector car—from classified ads to auctions—it's essential to understand the proper procedures each medium requires to make the right decisions. Knowing the mechanics of how each works, and by developing the correct game plan, you can save considerable time and effort in the quest for the "perfect" car.

If you're buying long distance, you may want to consider using an automobile transportation service, such as Intercity Lines, Inc.

LOCATION

Obviously, the ideal situation is to find a car nearby. This allows you to personally inspect and drive the car.

If the car is within 500 miles, be willing to take a weekend and drive the distance to see it. Take a friend, or better yet, someone who is knowledgeable about the car you are seeking. If the car sounds right, you know the seller has a solid reputation in the hobby, and the car is in concours condition, go ahead and take a trailer to bring your prize home. Of course, it is a lot easier to buy a car if it is nearby. You can see it, you can have someone check it out with you and a lot of logistical problems are eliminated. Many collectors find their cars within 500 miles of home, and for the right car at the right price, it's the easiest way to get started in the hobby.

AUCTIONS

You can find when and where auctions are held by looking in *Hemmings Motor News* or by checking the events calender in *Old Cars Weekly*. As a bidder, you will

To buy at an auction, you must register as a Bidder prior to the event. The auction company will send you a Bidder's registration packet. After filling it out and sending it in, you'll receive your Bidder's card.

Prior to the auction, you'll have time to inspect the cars and decide which ones you'd like to bid on. Try to determine the authenticity, condition, and what Reserve, if any, was placed on the car by the seller.

have to register with the auction company prior to the event. The auction company will send you a packet of information that includes a registration form. After you read and fill out the Bidder's registration form, send it back to the auction company along with the appropriate fee. You will then get your Bidder's card.

Methods of Payment—Besides the usual personal information (name, address, phone) you will be asked how you will pay for the car(s) you intend to buy. You will also be advised of the accepted methods of payment. Cash, of course, presents the least problem except perhaps when the sale is for a very large sum, and it's simply not advisable to carry amounts in the five figures on your person. Cashier and Certified Checks are also acceptable but don't feel offended if the seller or auction company calls the bank for verification, because even Certified checks can be stopped. These checks will most often be made out in the name of the buyer who will then endorse them over to the seller. Traveler's Checks are also acceptable as are currently dated Bank Letters of

The cars should have a tag similar to this one, which lists the car's auction number, and the day and time it is scheduled to go through the auction block.

Guarantee. When you register as a bidder you'll be asked to deposit this letter with the auction company.

If your bid on a car is accepted, then you will pay the money in one of either two ways. The first is called the Direct method of payment. When it is time to consum-

After inspecting the car you plan to bid on, join the other bidders as the cars move through the auction line. Observe how the auctioneer describes each car, and how others bid on them so you'll be ready when your car reaches the block.

mate the deal, the buyer will pay the seller directly, in the presence of an auction company clerk. In the Indirect method, if you are the buyer, you will pay the auction company who then will pay the seller.

At The Auction

When you receive your Bidder's card, you will also get a current list of the cars entered at the auction. Some cars may not arrive, while additional cars may be entered on the day of the auction. The list will give you the order in which the cars will be brought onto the auction block, so it is important to study it beforehand so that you don't miss bidding on the car(s) you are interested in.

Inspection—Arrive early so that you can locate the cars you're planning to bid on and inspect them. Perhaps the Corvette you wanted to bid on has a terrible paint job or another car caught your eye instead. The more time you allow for this, the better. Remember, too, that the inspec-

tion will be very limited. You can't test drive the car, you can't put it on a lift and if the owner isn't around, you can't even open the hood or the doors to get a better look inside. You can at least get an idea of how it runs when it is on the auction line. This is why some collectors are leery of buying at auctions. Unless the car is well known in the hobby (because it has won prestigious trophies, such as in the case of a Corvette winning Bloomington Gold Certification) it's difficult to verify authenticity and equally difficult to determine the car's true condition.

Authenticity—What about a car purchased at auction that turns out to be misrepresented or not authentic? Some auctions companies will negate the sale if it is found that an impropriety exists, however, in most cases, it is "buyer beware." The auction companies cannot guarantee the authenticity of a particular car. It is up to you to inspect the car prior to bidding, to satisfy yourself that the car is authentic. Just like with a private transaction, talk to the

Here's the GTO you've always wanted! But don't get caught up in bidding fever and forget your budget. When bidding, you may want to let someone else go first. If no one bids at the first price asked for, the auctioneer will sometimes start with a lower bid to get it going.

seller about the car and the car's history, but most important, it is up to you to know beforehand what to look for. If you have the slightest doubt, pass on the car. There will always be others.

Bidding—After you've found a car that you plan to bid on, join the other bidder's and watch the cars move through the auction. As each car comes up to the block, the auctioneer will read a description, and it's not unusual for them to embellish the car's good points. Remember, the auction company is interested in selling and will hype the cars strongly. They will try and start the bidding high, at least at the reserve level if the car has a reserve. If there are no takers, they will lower the price until someone bids. Then they will try to raise the bids incrementally until there are no more bids. Hopefully, there won't be many other bidders to drive the price up. Be aware that some auction companies employ "shills" that pose as bidders and are there to escalate the bidding.

If your's is the high bid and the seller accepts it, you have bought yourself a car! All that remains is to make payment and take care of the paperwork. The documentation is fairly straightforward, with the title changing hands as well as any other documentation that is required by law, such as an odometer statement, Bill of Sale, etc. Don't ask for a Bill of Sale that indicates a lower purchase price in order to save sales tax because you won't get it. Check all the paperwork for correctness, verifying VIN, mileage and other pertinent information. Take your time examining the paperwork—mistakes do happen.

Once the transaction is completed, the only thing left is to transport the car home. As most auctions are held on weekends, you'll have to wait until Monday to get a temporary plate from the local motor vehicle office unless the auction company has a tag and title clerk on the premises; this is also predicated on getting insurance coverage prior to arriving at the auction. You're better off

SELLING AT AUCTION

With the number of auctions going on across the country, chances are one will be close to you. Check the calender of events and auction ads in *Hemmings* and *Old Cars Weekly*. Call the auction company and have them send you an entry form. Fill out the form and return it along with the appropriate entry fee and a photocopy of your title. There is also a line on the entry form asking you to state if there are any liens on the vehicle. If there are, fill in the required information listing the amount of the lien and lienholder. The auction company can then verify the lien and, if the car should sell, deduct it from the sale amount. If there is no lien on the car, make sure that it says so on the title. If past liens have been satisfied, bring along the lien release forms provided by the lienholder. When the auction company receives your entry form, you will be assigned a sale number and a spot in the auction line.

Fees—Most auctions require a non-refundable fee for entering your car. These fees vary, depending on the auction itself and on the day that you want the car to be auctioned. Large, highly promoted auctions which attract many people will usually have higher overall entry fees. Because there are usually more bidders during certain days, the entry fees will be higher on those days.

Commissions—In addition to entry fees, auction companies charge a commission based on a percentage of the car's selling price. These can either be a *straight commission*, that is a fixed percentage of the selling price or on a graduated percentage basis in which the percentage charge declines as the selling price increases. Naturally, if the car is not sold, there is no commission to pay.

Some auctions will also charge a Buyer's Commission based on a percentage of the selling price. Here the Buyer pays commission in addition to the selling price. Make sure you find out if this is in effect. Commission rates can also vary if the car is offered with *Reserve* or with *No Reserve*. When a car is entered with a reserve, the seller has set a minimum price at which a car will be sold. Most cars entered at auctions are with reserve. If bidding does not reach this minimum, the seller is not obliged to sell. With no reserve, the seller is willing to accept the highest bid. The commission fee is based on the gross selling price and the entry fee doesn't apply to any commission. Obviously,

most sellers will add to their reserve price to cover any commission. Because it is riskier to sell with no reserve, most auction companies charge a smaller commission. There may also be other fees that the auction company will collect at the time of sale. Some states require the company to collect sales tax.

Preparation—You should prepare your car for the auction the same way as you would for any buyer—thoroughly detail the car and make sure it's in the best possible condition. Depending on where the auction is located, it may be a good idea to trailer the car there rather than driving it. You minimize the possibility of break down and the car will be cleaner upon arrival.

Setting Sale Price—At this point you should have already decided upon an asking price for the car and what reserve you'll put on it, if any. Of course, this can be changed at any time prior to your car going on the block. Before determining price, consider all the costs involved in placing the car in an auction. Along with the commission fee schedule that the auction company charges, factor in the costs incurred getting the car to the auction, meals, lodging and transportation back if the car sells. These costs quickly add up and they should always be included in your calculations.

Another factor in determining your price is the reserve itself. Many sellers enter their cars in auctions with unrealistic reserves and end up disappointed when the bidding doesn't reach their figure. Too many sellers overvalue their cars, while others are merely testing the market to see what kind of bids their car attracts. By setting a very high reserve the prospective seller can find out how much someone will bid and thus is in a better position when he tries to sell it privately. Even if you have set a reserve on your car, you can always drop it if you decide to sell during the bidding. All you have to do is tell the auctioneer that you'll accept the highest bid after the bidding stops. Auctioneers usually ask the seller if they would consider dropping the reserve in order to sell the car.

When you arrive at the auction to register, you will be asked to submit your title and any other state forms. You will be given a sticker to put on your windshield which describes your car, includes your car's Sale Number and also states the date your car is going on the block. After registration, park your car along with the other entered cars and wait for the auction to begin.

When checking out classified ads, ask plenty of the right questions. This Aston Martin may sound great in the ad, but as you can see, it needs quite a bit of restoration work.

bringing a trailer with you to the auction and trailering the car home, which also has the advantage of eliminating the possibility of breaking down on the way home or getting involved in an accident.

Advantages & Disadvantages

For the buyer, an auction is a great place to see a large variety of collector cars. Generally, the more prestigious the event, the better the quality, with cars being fully restored or close to it. Auctions, to a large degree, set the market prices for collector cars. If you are a conscientious, careful buyer and don't get caught into a bidding war with someone for a particular car, you can pay a "fair" price and drive away with a great deal.

On the other hand, auctions can be a dangerous place for the uninitiated. You'd better be able to make quick decisions. You can't test drive a car before bidding. You can't have a mechanic look at it, nor can you go home and "think about it." Most important, you have to keep a very cool head if the bidding gets hot. You don't want to get involved in a bidding war and end up paying too much. That's great for the seller, but bad for your wallet.

Many of the highly publicized auctions are geared more for the prewar classics and exotics. Look at the results of any recent auction and you'll see that the high dollars are going for the very rare investment grade cars—cars which are too valuable to drive anymore. A 1950s or 1960s Corvette or musclecar may be in the top ten, but interest in more mundane cars may not be as good. You may be able to pick up a bargain.

CLASSIFIED ADS

When responding to a classified ad, it is important to be direct. Ask if the car advertised is still available and then inquire if this is a good time to ask a few questions about the car. If there's a reason why the seller can't talk about the car at length when you call, ask when it will be convenient to call back and then do so at the agreed time.

Questions To Ask

As you talk to the seller, verify that you are both talking about the same car—the seller may have other cars for sale or there may have been a misprint on the ad. Ask him how long he has had the car and ask him why he is selling it. Ask what options and special features the car has. Inquire about the condition of the engine, interior, paint and other mechanical components. Has the engine been rebuilt? How is the transmission? Has the car ever been hit? How are the tires? Is there any rust?

Ask if the seller belongs to any clubs and if the car has won awards at any shows. Is the car modified from stock in any way? Is the engine "hopped-up?" Is there any custom bodywork on the car? Is the car presently registered and on the road or has it been sitting in a garage or other storage area?

If the car is damaged, determine what is wrong and ask if the seller has gotten any estimates on what it would cost to effect repairs. If repairs were done, inquire who made them and if receipts were kept.

Ask the seller what areas of the car aren't quite 100%. For example, it may not have original or reproduction tires but rather a modern set of radials. To some this isn't a big deal, but to other buyers there will be the additional expense of buying original type tires. The seller may tell you that anything that is needed is already taken into account in the selling price.

Let the seller talk freely about each question you've asked, rather than skipping back and forth between subjects. All you have to do is to direct the flow. It is also important that you take notes during this "interview" process.

PRICE

When you come down to it, price is the most important criterion by which you measure condition, rarity, desirability and so-on. Discussing price by long distance on a car you haven't seen is risky business. If the car sounds great and you think that the car may just be the one, this is the time to establish a tentative selling price. When you talk to the seller about price, tell him that any price you agree upon is subject to seeing the car in person. If the seller has stated his asking price in the ad, you may want to ask him if there is any flexibility on the price, or if the price is set in stone. If you don't like to dicker, ask him point-blank what's the lowest he'll take. A seller should know what he wants for his car—for that reason never make an offer on a car the seller hasn't set a price on.

If you're answering an ad that doesn't state a price, after the introductory formalities, ask the seller what he wants for the car. There is no point in wasting your time asking him questions just to find out that the price is out of line or just too much. If the price is too high for your budget, thank him for his time and tell him you'll get back to him if you haven't found something more in your range. You should also leave your name and number. You may be pleasantly surprised to receive a call later on.

Best Offer—What about an ad that asks for "best offer?" These situations require strategy. It's like a poker game—someone is holding good cards while the other may be bluffing. Throw the ball back into the seller's court and ask him what is the highest offer he has received so far. A seller should know what he wants for the car. When he quotes you the highest offer he's received, ask him if he has gotten a deposit yet. If he has, he should have told you up front that another party has put down a deposit. You can also make an offer that is deliberately too low in order to draw the seller out.

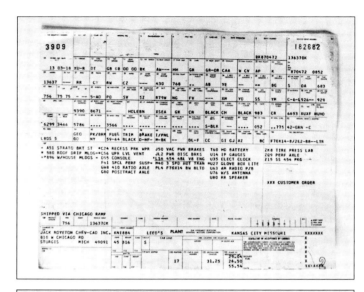

If the ad says "documented" or "original paperwork" these items are what it should include. From upper left, they are: The vehicle's "build sheet" or "broadcast sheet" which includes all factory codes, ship dates, where and when it was built, option codes and all body numbers which should correspond with those on the car; the original dealer invoice (left), which should include the VIN, color codes and option codes; and the original window sticker of the car (above).

Long Distance Buying

If the price is within your budget and the car sounds good, but it is too far away to run right over and take a look at it, the next step is to request that the seller send you several photos of the car, or better yet, ask for a videotape. You should always promise (or at least offer) to send them back if you don't buy the car.

When you receive the photos or tape, you have to decide whether you want to pursue this deal or not. If the car isn't the one, send the photos back with a polite note saying that you're not interested in the car. You'll probably get a call from the seller first, asking if you got the photos and what you think about them. If you do like the car, advise the seller when you'll be able to consummate the deal. If you can make the trip fairly soon (within a few days), then your intent to meet is a fairly good commitment on your part that you intend to make the purchase. **Deposits**—What complicates matters at this point is if

the price is really good, someone who won't bother waiting for photos might beat you to the car. What if you can't meet with the seller for two weeks or more? The possibility of someone else beating you to the car exists, especially if the market for that particular type of car is hot. Your intent to meet in several weeks is not enough to hold the car. Sure, you may find a seller that you've developed a close rapport with who'll hold the car, but generally, you'll need something more—a non-refundable deposit will secure the car for you. If you don't like the non-refundability aspect of it, you might as well realize that a refundable deposit is only as good as Monopoly money because it isn't securing anything. The seller is risking the possibility of turning away other cash buyers if you decide not to show up. Remember that the seller would rather follow through with the deal. Naturally, you'll want to make the deposit as small as reasonably possible.

What if, when you finally arrive, the seller misrepresented the condition of the car, and it's actually a

COLLECTOR CAR FINANCING

Banks are generally cautious about financing collector cars. With a new car, banks and other lending institutions require a minimum of documentation. Usually a credit application is all that is needed. Banks are generally more likely to take some risk with a new car because of the stated value, the ability to repossess it if the borrower defaults (the same applies to collector cars, too) and they are usually financing an amount that is less than the car's value.

With a collector car, there is generally a lot more paperwork involved. The lending institutions want to make sure that you are financially sound. For example, Midbanc, one of the larger collector car financing institutions, also requires that the borrower fill out a Personal Financial Statement. Here, assets, liabilities, all sources of income, real-estate holdings, life insurance policies and business venture information must be listed in addition to the usual credit information. In addition, detailed proof of income is stipulated, requiring that you submit copies of your tax returns for the last two tax years along with associated schedules. Unlike loans for a new car, you must be very detailed about your financial condition and credit history.

Other general guidelines stipulate that a borrower's income should be 2-1/2 to 3 times the amount financed and that the annual expenditures, including any new car payments, should not exceed 40-45% of income. In addition, the prospective borrower should have an excellent credit history and have financed similar amounts in the past. In other words, you'd better be very healthy financially. A final stipulation, a least with Midbanc, is that there is a minimum amount that can be financed, which is $15,000. Other lending sources have different minimums and maximums. The most common loan is a simple interest loan ranging from one to 20 years.

Many buyers who own their home can use a home equity loan to purchase their collector car. The advantage of the home equity loan is the interest is tax deductible and it's not necessary to jump through as many hoops to procure the funds as a bank loan.

candidate for the crusher? To protect your interests, submit your personal check as a deposit with the following statement written on the back: "*The endorsement of this check constitutes agreement of all terms and conditions made in connection with this sale.*" On the front of the check write "Deposit on car (year/model & serial #)." Along with your check, include a letter stating how long the deposit is to hold the year, make and model of the car, its serial number and the tentative amount you've agreed upon. Also state the date that you're planning to arrive and send it Certified Mail, Return Receipt requested. Your cashed check is your receipt for the deposit.

Long Distance Inspection—You can minimize your risk by having someone else inspect the car for you before you arrive. If you belong to a national car club, a local club official may be willing to look the car over for you. In fact, the local club may be familiar with the car and the seller—information that may help you to determine whether to buy from this individual or not. An alternative is to check the yellow pages. Most garages will accept credit cards over the phone and will agree to inspect the car for you. Remember that a mechanic can determine mechanical and even body damage, but chances are he won't be able to check matching numbers or be able to read a data plate. If the car is to be totally restored, mechanical and body damage—while important—is not as critical as ensuring that the correct engine and drivetrain are intact.

Final Details—Before you depart to see the car, call the seller and reconfirm your arrival date and time, taking into account any time zone differences. Verify with the seller that the car's paperwork is ready and in order and that all the spare parts (if any) are ready. Also make sure the car has a good spare tire and jack.

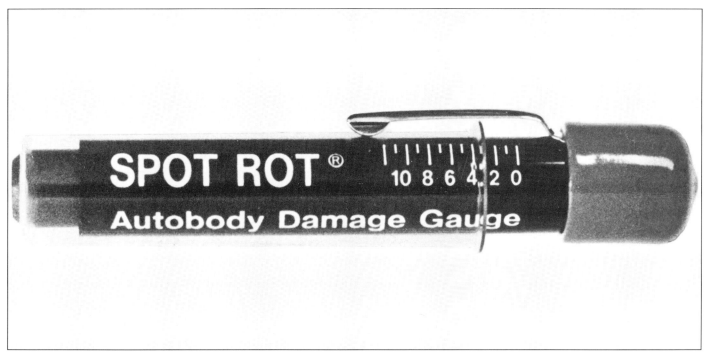

For exterior inspection, you should consider bringing this handy gadget. The Spot Rot gauge will detect just what lies underneath the paint. The magnet is placed on the body, and the gauge is pulled. A "10" indicates one paint job on solid metal. A "6-9" reading shows repainting, while a "1-5" reading warns of hidden rust or collision damage. To obtain one, contact Pro Motorcar Products, 22025 U.S. 19 North, Clearwater, FL 34625. 800/323-1090.

Finally, reconfirm the price. Advise the buyer you are assuming he's represented the car correctly and the price agreed on is based upon the car as described. Advise him that your offer may change once you've had a chance to examine the car yourself. If he disagrees or argues, suggest to him that you may cancel the deal. If he's been honest with you, the seller should be agreeable to your terms. If he's misrepresented the car, now is the time to decide whether to proceed further.

THE INSPECTION

The hardest part, regardless of where the car is located, is determining its condition. As a guide, you can use the checklist on page 42 for the inspection. If you are mechanically inclined, chances are you probably won't need the services of a mechanic to check out the car. If you aren't that knowledgeable, the modest cost involved in hiring a mechanic is well worth it. The important thing here is not to feel embarrassed or intimidated, even if you know that you are looking at an absolutely perfect car. As a buyer, it is your right to inspect the car. At the same time, don't get so excited that you overlook defects. This happens often to novices who think they have found the car of their dreams; they're so busy thinking of what

they'll be doing with the car when they get it home that they are bound to overlook something critical. It's essential to keep cool and objective. It doesn't hurt to bring an objective friend along to keep your enthusiasm in check.

Exterior Inspection

Examine the car from every angle, looking for any waves in the body panels which could indicate poor bodywork. Check for differences in paint color, texture and uniformity which indicates that the car has been repainted, and also take care to look for panel fit. Is the gap between the doors and fenders even or is there more space in one area than another? Again, this is a sign that the car

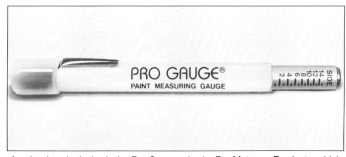

Another handy device is the Pro Gauge, also by Pro Motorcar Products, which can measure the thickness of paint on the car to .001 inch. It enables you to measure the paint on a car to be certain if it has been repainted, or to determine how long the current paint job may last.

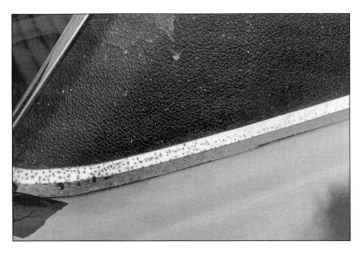

Some defects are easy to spot. Pitted chrome trim will have to be either refinished or replaced.

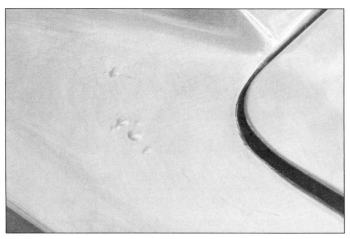

Paint bubbling indicates rust underneath the paint. If it's so obvious here, where else may it be lurking?

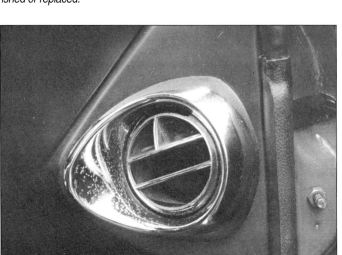

Notice the pitting; this means to obtain a flawless finish, the vent will have to be removed and rechromed or replaced.

has had bodywork done. Pay close attention to the lower body areas which are susceptible to rust. Look under the doors for rust, too. Any rust is too much, even slight surface rust. For example, if there is a little spot of rust on the door, the proper way to repair it would be to remove the rust and have the entire door panel repainted. Even the best painters can't color match an entire panel.

Trunk & Interior

Don't forget to open the trunk and look under the spare. If there is a trunk mat, lift it and inspect underneath it for any damage or rust. Be thorough in the interior, too. Look for excessive wear on the pedals, seat surfaces and carpets. Make sure that everything works—wipers, radio, air conditioning, as well as all the gauges. If they don't work,

it means that you'll have to pay to have them repaired or replaced and should be taken into account when you bring up the subject of price with the seller. Be wary of a odometer that doesn't work or a "stuck" odometer—this could mean that the car has many more miles than what is indicated on the odometer. If the car is a convertible, make sure that the top mechanism functions properly. Look for tears and rips—the top should go up and down easily, without catching, and it should latch securely. Check the well behind the rear seat for water stains or rust, and make sure the hydraulic system isn't leaking.

Engine Inspection

Next, look at the all-important engine compartment. You can sometimes tell if the engine compartment has been recently steam-cleaned if small patches of paint are missing from the engine. The pressure and heat from the steam removes the dirt and grime but also removes old, dried-out paint too. This could mean that the seller, rather than maintaining a clean engine, had it recently steam-cleaned to make a better impression on any prospective buyer. Look for telltale signs, such as silicone sealer overflowing from the manifold or cylinder heads, which would indicate that the engine has been recently rebuilt. Remove the oil dipstick and note the color of the oil. A dark color indicates that the oil hasn't been changed in a while. If the oil is milky white, there is water leakage—possibly a bad head gasket or a cracked cylinder head or block. At this time, check the condition of the engine's belts, hoses, wires and battery. You don't want something minor to fail if you drive the car home.

This interior appears to be in good shape. However, there are minor flaws that will be revealed upon closer inspection.

This seatback is beginning to show some wear, and it won't be long before it splits, necessitating new seat covers.

Now it's time to start the engine, if it can be started. If in tune, the engine should start relatively quickly. Listen for any unusual noises, uneven idle, hissing or clanking sounds. If the engine cranks very slowly, but then catches, it could mean that either the battery is weak, the starter is bad, the timing is off or that there may be an electrical problem. Either way, it shows that something is wrong, because anyone who is showing the car to a prospective buyer, would make sure that everything is working properly—unless the buyer is unloading a collectible that needs work. You'll also be able to tell at this point if the car needs a muffler or not.

If the car is equipped with an oil pressure gauge, note how high the pressure reads. If the pressure initially reads high but then drops and stays low, it may be that very heavy oil is used to disguise a worn engine. While the engine is running, remove the oil filler cap. If you see smoke puffing out, you can be sure that it is a worn engine because there is just too much blow-by getting past the rings. The engine may run all right, but it will use a lot of oil and its days are numbered. If an engine rebuild is not in your plans for restoration, think twice about buying a car with a tired powerplant.

While you still have the hood up, if the car is equipped with an automatic transmission, check the transmission fluid. The fluid should be red or pink. Smell the fluid on the stick. Does it have a burnt smell? If the fluid is burnt, the condition of the transmission may be in question.

Also check the power steering reservoir, if there is one.

Since automatic transmission fluid is used here, a dark, burnt fluid indicates two things. First, that the power steering pump is going and also that the owner may not have included the power steering pump in his maintenance schedule—a clue that other components may also have been overlooked.

Road Testing

As you drive the car, listen for any unusual noises. Is there a loud "clunk" when you shift the transmission to Drive on an automatic? This can indicate bad U-joints. On a manual transmission, note when the clutch engages and perform a stall test by putting it in first gear and letting the clutch out slowly without your foot depressing the accelerator. A good clutch will stall the engine as it is released. Also, start the car in third gear. If the engine revs too high in relation to the speed the car is moving, it indicates that the clutch is slipping.

Note any inconsistencies when you drive. Does the engine hesitate, ping or backfire? On an automatic transmission-equipped car, does the transmission shift smoothly without hanging up between shifts? If it's a musclecar from the 1960s, it should live up to its image, exhibiting almost effortless acceleration and excellent throttle response.

See if the car pulls to one side or another while cruising and also during braking. If it pulls as you are driving along, it could either mean that the front suspension is out of alignment, indicating the need for an alignment or suspension repairs or that one of the tires is under-

The carpet along the bottom of the door panel obviously needs to be replaced. Again, a minor flaw that will need to be fixed, but one that shouldn't keep you from buying the car. Flaws like this can be used as bargaining chips when negotiating the price.

Be sure to check under the carpets to examine the floor. If you find a gaping rust hole like this, you better do some serious thinking. A hole like this can only be repaired one of two ways. The first is to cut the rust area out and weld in sheet metal to cover it. The other is to replace the entire floorpan of the car. Both options are expensive. Again, finding rust damage like this should make you look closely for more, such as in the frame and wheelwells.

inflated. If it pulls while braking, it indicates that the brakes are grabbing and will need to be adjusted or replaced.

Sometimes suspension problems don't show up at slow speeds; make sure you bring the car up to a decent cruising speed—at least 55 mph. Take some fast turns and note how the car reacts. Is there excessive body lean? This could mean that the shock absorbers or springs are bad. There shouldn't be any unusual noises as you drive, corner and brake. Noises indicate problems.

Does the rear axle whine as you accelerate or decelerate? It can be a sign of ring and pinion trouble as can rear axle clunking noises as you corner, which could be a bad limited slip differential.

As you are driving, check to see that all the accessories work, such as the radio, turn signals, windshield wipers, heater fan, air conditioner and any other power accessories. Drive with the windows up. Do you hear any whistling or wind noise? This can indicate that the weatherstripping is worn.

Now have the seller drive the car as you follow it from behind. Look at the exhaust pipes and note the color of the exhaust. Blue smoke indicates bad rings or valve guides while black smoke indicates that the carburetor is too rich. White smoke, after the car has been fully warmed up, is a very bad sign as it indicates that water

is getting into the combustion chambers. A cracked cylinder block, head or head gasket is the cause.

Also note how the car tracks and reacts when it is braking and cornering as the seller drives it. Look to see if anything underneath the car is hanging precariously as it is being driven and also see if you can spot any fluids leaking.

After you've completed the test drive, lift the hood and look for any leaks. Then restart the car. It should start right up. Move the car enough to see if any fluids leaked in the meantime and also check the gauges just to make sure that the engine is functioning correctly.

If you can, take the car to a local service station and ask them to put it on a lift. It is much easier to spot any leaks, damage, and rust while the car is in the air.

Decision Time

If the car requires more work then you're willing to invest, back out of the deal now, because problems can arise if the car isn't quite what the seller represented it to be. Bring these things to the seller's attention and tell him that after seeing the car that you don't feel comfortable enough to complete the transaction and that you want your deposit refunded, if you sent him one. You sent him the deposit in good faith based on his representation of the car. That is why it is important to include the letter

If the engine looks like this, obviously you'll have to consider serious rebuilding and detailing costs. This may give you some leverage to bargain with price.

On the other hand, an engine like this means the owner is a serious enthusiast and has probably maintained the car well. However, always check the engine to make sure it is in good running condition—no matter how good it looks. Photo courtesy Musclecar Review.

While you are road testing, listen for any unusual noises, such as pings, backfires or whines from the drivetrain. Noises like these mean trouble. Also, see how the car handles and brakes.

Excessive body lean during cornering may indicate poor shocks. Look for this condition while road testing.

with your deposit along with the statement written on the back of the check.

If the car doesn't check out to your satisfaction but you still want it, advise the seller the problem areas you've found indicate the need for repairs and thus warrants a lower price. The seller may ask you what you're willing to pay or he may tell you that he'll have the problem areas repaired. If you can reach an agreement suitable to both parties, the sale can be completed.

THE FINAL TRANSACTION

How should you pay for the car? The most common method is by a Cashier's check or a Certified check. However, the seller may not want to receive checks for over $10,000 dollars and may request several checks. Paying by cash is not recommended for obvious reasons. Have the check(s) made out to both yourself and the seller, which requires your endorsement for the check to be cashed. When paying for the car, you can also avoid a lot of difficulties if you make the Cashier's check you brought along for 85-90% of the previously agreed upon selling price. That way, if the car isn't what it was represented to be, but you still want it, there won't be any trouble when you renegotiate the selling price; you can pay the balance in Traveler's checks. You won't be stuck giving the seller the original amount and then taking his check back for the difference or any other agreement that opens the possibility of loss for you.

Documents—Have the title signed over to you and have a Bill of Sale made up. You can use the one in the sidebar nearby as a guide.

Clear title is essential to making the purchase. Check with your local motor vehicle office on what documentation you'll need from the seller to register the car once you get it home. Usually the title and Bill of Sale is all that is required, but you should verify this with the motor vehicle office.

Liens—What if there is a lien holder? If there is a lien shown on the title, call the bank in question and ask them the amount owed on the car, then have the seller give you a letter addressed to the bank authorizing them to release the title to you, upon payment of balance on the loan. You can deduct this from the amount you bought the car for and then pay it directly to the bank; or, you can have the seller do it. The bank will then either show that the lien

is satisfied on the title itself or it may give you a lien release form or letter. Don't treat the matter of liens lightly. Don't take the seller's word that the title is good, even though the lien on it doesn't show that it is satisfied.

Parts—If there are parts included in the deal, make sure you get them right then and there. Unless you absolutely trust that the seller will ship them to you as agreed, it is better that you make your own arrangements—one less thing to worry about.

Transporting—Finally, if you intend to drive the car back, make sure you've contacted the local motor vehicle office regarding temporary plates and inspections. Listed in the appendix are the phone numbers of each state's title bureaus. Also, it is in your best interest to have the car insured before you pick it up. If you are trailering the car back, you don't need to get it registered, but you should still get some form of insurance.

SAMPLE DOCUMENTS

RECEIPT OF DEPOSIT
I, (Your Name), have received from (Buyers Name) $ as deposit for the purchase of 1969 Boss 429 Mustang serial # 9F02Z171618 until October 22, 1991.
DATE:
SIGNED:
WITNESS:

Make at least two copies, keep one and send one to the person making the deposit.

BILL OF SALE
I,(Your Name), hereby sell and transfer title and legal ownership of (Year, make, model & serial number) to (name of Buyer) for the sum of $_____.
There are no liens or encumbrances on this vehicle except those in favor of: (Name and address of lienholder—if none state N/A)
DATE:
SELLER:
BUYER:
NOTARY:

Inspection Checklist

ENGINE

Starter
Slow____ Noisy____

Engine Idle
Unchanged____ Uneven____ Run-on after shutting down____

Acceleration
Smooth____ Flat spots____ Surging____ Pinging____ Unusual noises____ Misfiring____
High rpm acceleration—strong & even?____

EXHAUST SYSTEM
Unusual noises____ Excessive muffler noise____

INSTRUMENTS
Normal readings____ Abnormal readings____

DRIVETRAIN

Manual Transmission
Excessive noise____ Shifter won't stay in gear____ Gears grinding____ Won't get in gear____ Clutch slips____
High/low clutch pedal____

Automatic Transmission
RPM increase during shifts (slippage) ____ Shifts hard____ Shifts too soon____ Shift delayed____
Excessive clunking while putting in gear____

Rear Axle
Whine during acceleration____ Whine during deceleration____
Clunking during cornering____

Driveshaft
Vibration____ Loose U-Joints____

BRAKES
Unusual noises and grinding____ Pulls to one side____ Hard pedal____ soft pedal____ spongy pedal____
Pulsating pedal____

Parking Brake
Doesn't hold car in place____ Doesn't release smoothly____

STEERING & SUSPENSION
Car pulls to one side____ Car wanders____ Steering wheel doesn't return to center after a turn____
Unusual noises during turning____ Excessive body lean____ Excessive front-end dive during braking____
Wheels hit body/suspension components during turning____
Excessive steering wheel movement over bumps____ Excessive body movement over bumps____
Tire vibration/unbalanced tires____ Tires showing uneven wear____

INTERIOR
Wind noise____ Floor drafts____ Rattles/noises____ Windows don't go up/down smoothly or completely____
Doors don't close properly____ Vents don't work____ Blower fan doesn't work____ Heater doesn't get hot____
A/C doesn't blow cold____ Heater/A/C control panel switches don't work____ Speedometer doesn't work____
Speedometer cable noisy____ Odometer doesn't work____ Gauges that don't work____
Turn signals/warning flashers malfunctioning____ Power Seats____ Power windows____ Power door locks____
Power trunk release____ Radio/tape player____ Wipers____ Lighter____

INSURANCE FOR COLLECTOR CARS

3

Insuring your collector car is absolutely essential. However, you'll need a different type of policy than you usually get for your daily driver.

Insurance is required by law on every vehicle driven on public roads. It is designed to pay for property damage and bodily injury that may occur in the event of an accident. The differences between regular car and collector car insurance relate to how the vehicle damage is covered and consideration for vehicle value.

With regular insurance issued by a standard carrier, the policy is written with the understanding that the vehicle will depreciate every year to the point that it is worth much less than when purchased new. This is known as *Actual Cash Value*. With Actual Cash Value, the amount paid by the insurance carrier is limited to the amount of the *actual loss*. This amount is determined by establishing the car's value before and after the damage—the difference between the two is the loss. Consequently, collision and comprehensive premiums are reduced each year on a policy as the vehicle depreciates. As the vehicle's depreciation curves downward, it drops to a point

where the cost of repair exceeds the value of the vehicle. For example, a 1980 Chevette involved in a rear end collision is worth far less than the cost to repair the damage. Consequently, the insurance company will write the car off as a total loss and issue a check for the book value. The damage incurred may cost $2,000 to repair; as a total loss, the insurance company will pay only several hundred dollars to cover the Chevette's book value.

The owner of a valuable collector car needs a special insurance policy. It must take into account the fact the vehicle is worth considerably more than book value, and that the standard books used to rate vehicle value are not correct when determining collector car values. Without specialized insurance for collector cars, it would be impossible to file a claim with a standard carrier and expect to be compensated for the vehicle's innate worth as a collectible.

Actual Cash Value (ACV) policies mean that there is no limit of liability to the insurance company. If the car is worth $35,000 when insured, but has appreciated to a value of $50,000 at the time of loss, then the insurance company is liable for the value at time of loss, in this case $50,000. With investment grade cars like the Cobra, this is the best policy to have. Also, it could work the other way. The car could depreciate from the purchase price, in which case you'd only be compensated for the lesser amount.

ACTUAL CASH VALUE (ACV)

This is the most common type of insurance coverage available for regular vehicles. For the typical daily-driven car, the insured doesn't have to prove what the car is worth before the policy is written; the policy states that the insurance company is only liable for ACV at the time of loss. This is fine for most newer cars which rapidly depreciate—there are numerous industry price guides. But it can create problems if the insured car is *appreciating* in value. In this situation, it is up to the insured to prove to the insurance company the car's value.

Advantages

The advantage of an ACV policy is there is no limit to the amount of liability on the part of the insurance company. If a car is worth $25,000 when the policy is issued but has appreciated to $35,000 at time of loss, then the insurance company is liable for the $35,000. And if the owner has made considerable improvements on the car, such as major body and paint work or a new interior, the insurance coverage automatically increases because the car is worth more. This applies to cars that appreciate in

44

Stated Amount Coverage doesn't mean you'll get what you thought at time of loss. These types of policies generally come with a Limit of Liability clause. If the owner insures this '67 Corvette for $75,000 and the car is stolen, but the insurance company determines the car's worth at only $30,000 at the time of loss, the collector will only get $30,000. If the owner insures the Corvette for $15,000, he will only get that amount, even though the insurance company has valued the car at $30,000. Either way, it's a win-win situation for the insurance company.

value but again, it is up to the insured to prove to the insurance company that the car is worth more at time of loss. Proof comes in the form of a professional appraisal, keeping track of auction sales and assembling and updating a listing of what comparable cars are advertised for in newspapers and magazines.

STATED AMOUNT COVERAGE

The most common insurance policy written for collector cars is based on *Stated Amount*. Stated Amount policies are often misunderstood by collectors, who mistakenly believe the vehicle is insured for the value as determined by the owner at the time the policy is written. The insured pays premiums based on an amount that he establishes, thinking that if there is a loss, the insurance company is liable for that amount. This is not necessarily so.

Limits of Liability

What many policy holders aren't aware of (or don't understand) are several clauses found in most Stated Amount policies. These are usually grouped under what

is referred to as the *Limit of Liability* clause. In essence, these clauses stipulate that the limit of liability for loss will be the lesser of the stated amount shown in the *Declaration* or *Schedule*, actual cash value of the stolen or damaged property or the amount necessary to repair or replace the property.

This basically amounts to an ACV policy with a liability limit. If a collector insures his 1967 Corvette convertible for $75,000 and the car is stolen, he is not going to collect $75,000. If the insurance company determines the car is worth $30,000, based on an appraisal, current auction prices or other sources, then that is all the insured is going to collect.

Conversely, if the Corvette owner's policy states that the car is insured for $15,000, then the insurance company will pay only that amount and no more—not even the actual cash value, which in our example is $30,000. This is likely to happen if the insured fails to keep track of current prices.

Most collectors mistakenly believe that they are entitled to the stated amount on the policy, however a fundamental insurance principle states that an insured is

SPECIALTY INSURANCE RESTRICTIONS

Because of the lower premiums inherent with collector car insurance, there are numerous stipulations attached to the policy regarding the use of the insured vehicle. One of the major restrictions concerns mileage. Most policies limit use to 2,500 miles per year. Most carriers will waive this if the car is to be driven to a national event. The insured must apply for permission first and will be required to document the event, the distance and other information prior to written consent from the carrier.

Other restrictions include:

• The vehicle must be at least 15 years old.

• The vehicle is not to be used for general transportation. That includes an occasional drive to work or the grocery store or any place where the car will be left unattended.

• No participation in timed or racing events.

• Unless part of a collection, the vehicle must be kept in a fully enclosed, locked garage at the primary residence.

Other restrictions may apply regarding multiple car collections, cars valued in excess of $100,000, minimum accepted driver age and the insured's driving record. Restrictions will vary between insurance carriers.

entitled to be compensated only for the amount of the loss incurred and not profit from the insurance contract. Insurance is a contract of indemnity; paying the stated amount would in effect change it to a valued contract.

If in the event the customer has overvalued the vehicle on the application form, most insurance carriers will inquire why such a high value was placed on the vehicle and in most cases, will want the vehicle appraised. The reason why some cars are overvalued is that the collector has spent a lot of money on the restoration. A 1963 six-cylinder Plymouth Fury valued by the insured for $25,000 doesn't have a market value for that amount, even if $25,000 was spent to restore it. This is a point to remember when you're considering what car to buy and how much money will be required to restore it.

Does it make sense to purchase Stated Amount coverage when all the insured is going to collect is Actual Cash Value, provided it is less than the Stated Amount, especially when Stated Amount coverage costs more? Some may argue that Stated Amount coverage premiums, at least as they apply to collector cars, are less. But the lower premiums come with specific restrictions that must be followed for the insurance to remain in effect.

STATED VALUE COVERAGE

Also known as *Agreed Amount Coverage,* this sort of policy is difficult to obtain, although the typical collector thinks he is getting SVC when he fills out a specialty collector car insurance application form. SVC is used when it is difficult to establish a value at time of loss. The insurance company and the insured must agree, before the policy is written, on what the car is worth and this amount is stated on the policy. If there is a loss, the insurance company will pay the the stated amount or the amount necessary to repair or replace the car, *whichever is less.*

Stated Value Coverage generally requires an appraisal before the policy is approved and the insured is obligated to keep track of current pricing and adjust the stated value annually to keep the coverage in line with current market values. Most carriers will review the adjustment and will kick it back to the insured if they disagree.

Most collector cars are covered by Stated Amount Coverage polices because it's considerably cheaper than regular ACV insurance. For example, the premium for the maximum liability coverage ($300,000 at one of the larger insurers), will cost $32.00 per year on the typical collector car that is over 15 years old. Physical damage premium ranges from $.50 per $100 of valuation to $2.25 per $100.

Stated Value Coverage is difficult to obtain. With this policy, the insurance company and the insured must agree on what the car is worth before the policy is written. In case of loss, the insurance company will pay the stated amount or the amount necessary to repair or replace the car, whichever is less. This type of policy usually requires an appraisal prior to issuance of the policy.

SHOPPING FOR INSURANCE

The first place to shop for insurance is with your local agent. As the collector car hobby grew in the 1980s, many standard insurance agents and their insurance companies learned to write policies for special interest and collector cars. Don't stop at just one quote; check with several insurance companies and keep track of what each company offers and also note what exclusions and limitations there may be.

Most collectors end up with insurance provided by a specialty insurance company, such as American Collectors, J.C. Taylor or Condon & Skelly. These companies advertise in *Hemmings Motor News* and other collector publications. Most of these act as agents for an established insurance company and virtually all of the policies offered are of the Stated Amount type. Shop around and determine which company's restrictions best fit your needs.

Keep Accurate Records

However you insure your collectible, keep complete and accurate records. To ensure protecting the car's insured value, have it appraised and keep any articles that help to determine your car's value, including auction results and price guides. Presenting this information will make it much easier to prove your car's value in case of loss. Also keep all receipts of work done and photograph the car from various angles (submit copies to the insurance company) to prove condition. By making sure you can substantiate the value of your car should a loss occur, having the proper policy that fits your needs and insuring the vehicle for the right amount, you won't be disappointed later on if you have to file a claim.

Collector car insurance policies carry restrictions (see sidebar p. 46). In most cases, the car can only be driven a maximum of 2,500 miles per year, but not for general transportation purposes. This means it's okay to drive it at a car show but not to the grocery store. Photo by Michael Lutfy.

These two photos illustrate why insurance companies don't like racing. Even though this is a vintage car race, where drivers are supposed to take it "easy," the drivers of a Shelby Mustang and F-5000 car lose it in a turn and go off course. Photos by Michael Lutfy.

Driving your collector car in timed or racing events is forbidden by most insurance companies. Photo by Michael Lutfy.

BASIC RESTORATION TIPS 4

Depending on your mechanical aptitude, financial resources and overall desire, you should be able to perform all or part of the restoration yourself. Some areas, such as heavy body and paint work and complete engine rebuilding, might be better off with a professional if you don't have the proper space, tools and knowledge. But much of the joy of owning a collector car is in bringing out that "diamond in the rough" yourself.

When it comes to the actual nitty-gritty of restoring a car, some enthusiasts may choose to hire out some or all of the restoration work. Don't overestimate your abilities. Much of the decision will rest on your capabilities. If the car is extremely rough, you're better off farming out the body and paint work to a professional. If the car is straight and not in too bad a shape, there's no reason why you can't perform some of the work yourself. Part of the pleasure of owning a collector car is to restore it yourself; bringing the diamond out of the rough is a challenge that can be pleasurable as well as rewarding.

ORIGINAL VS MODIFIED

The first requirement is to understand exactly what the term "restoration" means: it is returning an automobile to its exact condition as it left the assembly line. Anything else is *not* a restoration. Call it a refurbishment, a rebuild or a renovation, but not a restoration. Altering the car in any way means it is *modified*. Modifications can take the form of improvements to the car's performance or its appearance. For example, a modification can be an update to the ignition system using electronic ignition conversion kits. Electronic ignition is much more reliable than the conventional points ignition that most pre-1970 cars have. Some people also prefer to have customized bodywork and paint on their cars—something which is definitely beyond the realm of originality.

Points to Consider

Understanding the rules before you play the game is essential. If you plan on entering the car in concours competition, then you'll have to go for strict originality, down to every original nut and bolt. It can be quite an expensive proposition to restore a car to its original state

Original or modified? That's the first question you have to answer before rebuilding your car. Obviously this '57 Chevy was heavily modified, to the point where it can not be put back to stock without a lot of major work. Photo by Michael Lutfy.

You're going to need proper space to work. Essentials are good lighting, heat, plenty of space for parts and tools and room to maneuver in. You'll also need plenty of 110- and 220-volt outlets.

because it requires a complete teardown and restoration from the "ground up." If you plan to build a fun driver, there's a lot more leeway with what you can do since you can add non-stock aftermarket parts to upgrade the car's handling and braking.

Save Original Parts—If you do chose to modify your collector car, save all the parts replaced and always try to make the modifications easily convertible. Thus, if you decide to install a different set of wheels, keep the old ones. The same applies if you install a larger carburetor, or update the ignition. If and when you decide to sell the car, you'll be able to attract more buyers because the market for original cars is much larger than the market for modified cars. Stay away from engine swaps and body modifications. Such modifications are a lot harder to reconvert to stock, should you decide to sell later on.

52

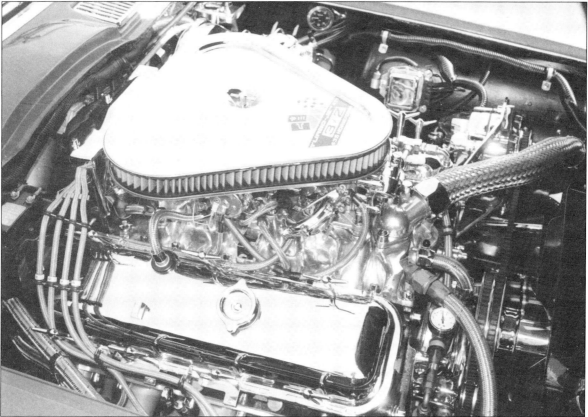

These photos illustrate two different approaches to rebuilding the engine compartment. The engine on top is restored to stock, original form. The one on the bottom has just about every conceivable nut and bolt chromed, plus a lot of aftermarket replacement parts. Which method you choose really depends on your taste, and whether or not you want an original or modified car. Photos by Michael Lutfy.

Along with basic tools (screwdrivers, pliers, wrenches, sockets, etc.) you'll need a variety of power and specialty tools. One of the best sources for these is The Eastwood Company. For a catalog, contact: The Eastwood Company, 580 Lancaster Ave., Box 296, Malvern, PA 19355. 800/345-1178.

Consider the Costs—Also consider the costs of restoring a car. It's easy to get over your head very quickly in the heated rush of buying and tearing down the car. Set a realistic budget and a timetable you can work with. Be prepared to exceed that budget and that timetable, because restorations rarely meet your first projections. One important consideration is whether the cost justifies the expense. For example, does it make much sense to invest $15,000 in a 1965 Valiant? Of course, there may be other reasons why someone would want to make such an investment, but future resale at a profit wouldn't be one of them.

PLANNING & PREPARATION

The first step in restoring your car is one that will ultimately save you time and money. It is essential that you spend time planning your restoration, from beginning to end. It is advisable that you do so on paper, perhaps making a flow chart of areas to be done, tools and parts that need to be purchased, what work is to be farmed out and what work you will do yourself. Paying attention to these details can make the difference between a fun, pleasurable experience and a veritable nightmare that seems to have no end.

Location

Brain surgery isn't performed on kitchen tables, and correct restorations aren't performed in driveways. You need to have a facility to store your project, all the parts and tools you need and a place to work. Even if you're not going to restore the car yourself, a garage is necessary, otherwise the car will continue to deteriorate if left out in the elements. Even the most basic garage must be well lit, have enough working space for parts and tools and if at all possible, it should be heated. It's not much fun working on a car when it's only 25 degrees outside. Regarding space, you need at least a two-car garage with plenty of bench space to disassemble, restore and reassemble components, room to paint and lots of storage space for parts.

Reference manuals specific to your car are a must. Some can be located at dealerships, others at swap meets or you may find them advertised in Hemmings Motor News. HPBooks and Classic Motorbooks also are fine sources.

It's best to get as many parts in advance before tearing down the car. If possible, you're better off getting originals and reconditioning them. Parts like this can be found through ads in Hemmings and Old Cars Weekly, or junkyards, swap meets and car shows. If you can't find originals, or don't want to bother with reconditioning them, you can generally buy the part from a reproduction parts business.

Along with sufficient space, you'll need plenty of 110- and 220-volt outlets. Overhead lamps are a necessity, and the walls should be painted white so your work area is bright. Also handy but not essential is running water and a large sink to clean parts in.

Tools

You can never have enough tools. At the very minimum you should have a complete set of hand tools. This should include 1/4-, 3/8- and 1/2-inch drive socket sets with several ratchets, extensions and the like and a breaker-bar. If you're planning to assemble your engine, you'll also need a torque wrench. Naturally, a good selection of screwdrivers, pliers and vice-grips is mandatory and you'll also need specialized tools if you're planning to work on the brakes and suspension. Even if you think you've got a good selection of tools already, there will

be times when you'll find yourself going to the hardware store to get a special socket or tool because you just can't get to that bolt with the sockets you've got. There are some tools or equipment you'll only have to use once or twice. You can stretch your budget by renting these tools instead of buying them.

If you're planning to work on components such as carburetors, certain specialized tools may be required. For example, some Holley carburetors require a special type of screwdriver to remove the carburetor's metering plates. If you're going to work on the electrical system, a test light, a voltmeter and an ohm meter are necessary.

Power Tools—Beyond hand-tools, a compressor is a another essential piece of equipment. Trying to pull a 25-year-old car apart with hand tools will take time and effort. Air tools will cut your work time in half. A compressor is also useful for cleaning parts and a necessity

A "ground-up" or "body-off" restoration means disassembling the entire car, and reconditioning, rebuilding and/or replacing all parts. With many older cars, this entails lifting the body off the frame, as shown here. Unibody cars can only have the suspension and engine removed, because they bolt directly to the body shell instead of to a separate frame.

if you're going to do any painting. If you are going to do much of the disassembly and restoration work yourself and if your budget allows, consider a sandblaster and a small glass beader. A sandblaster will strip rust and debris from cast parts such as exhaust manifolds, and a glass beader is a useful tool for cleaning rubber, aluminum and metal parts without altering the surface texture. It beats trying to wire-brush parts in a pail of mineral spirits. If you plan on using a sandblaster, make sure your compressor is at least 2.5 horsepower with a 20-gallon tank. Also, install a water separator to keep the air line to the sandblaster nozzle dry—wet sand can't cut rust and paint. If you decide to add equipment like this to your garage, you'll find The Eastwood Company (580 Lancaster Ave., Malvern, PA 19355 1-800-345-1178) to be a great source of supply. Call them to get their free catalog.

If you're not up to the task of performing the restoration yourself and have plenty of cash, you can simply drop off your car at a restoration shop. Concours Restorations, located in Rancho Cucamonga, CA, specializes in factory-correct restorations. Photo by Michael Lutfy.

This sight is a bit intimidating, but you knew the engine looked like this when you bought it, didn't you? All you can do is grab some tools and dig in. When you begin to despair, try to keep the end result in mind.

Reference Material—You can't restore a car without reference material. Start with a factory service manual. It will give all the correct specs, illustrate the proper methods to disassemble and assemble parts, plus the drawings and photos are very useful. Look in *Hemmings Motor News* under the "Books and Literature" section for vendors who specialize in manuals. Like everything else, it pays to shop around. There are also superb "how-to" handbooks from HPBooks, that can be purchased in many automotive retail outlets or through the Classic Motorbooks catalog.

Parts

You're going to replace a lot of parts during the course of a full-blown restoration. Where you locate and purchase them is dependent to a certain extent on how exact you want your restoration to be. Some original parts are still available from your local auto parts store, such as rings, bearings, camshafts, gasket sets, carburetor rebuild kits, water and oil pumps and the like. Depending on the year of your collector car, a surprising number of parts are still available from the manufacturer. Unfortunately, the countermen at some dealerships aren't interested in spending the time to look up part numbers for old cars, but you can help them by leaving a list and letting them look up the part numbers and checking for availability at their leisure. Finding a friendly counterman may take some time, but it can be worth the effort. And remember, it doesn't hurt to tip them for their time and effort. That will make it a lot easier when you go back in for your next orders.

Reproduction Parts—During the last 15 years or so, there has been a tremendous growth of companies that reproduce original parts for cars that would be considered collectible. Many companies specialize in particular makes, such as Chevelle Classics or Classic Camaro, and offer a complete line of restoration parts ranging from sheet metal to trim, interior soft parts to engine accessory brackets and emblems. These vendors can be found in *Hemmings* and many enthusiast magazines as well as national club newsletters.

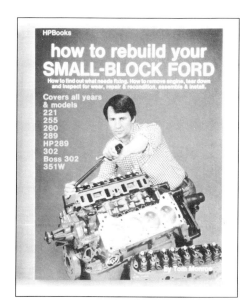

HPBooks has rebuild manuals available for most Ford, Chevy and Chrysler engines, both big and small block. For a free catalog, contact Price Stern Sloan, Attn: Customer Service, 11150 Olympic Blvd., Sixth Floor, Los Angeles, CA 90064. 800/421-0892.

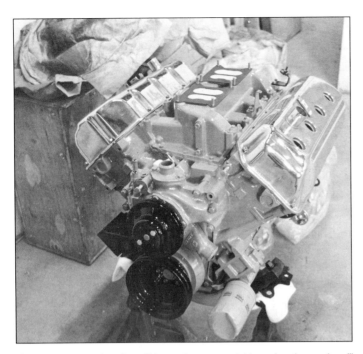

Of course, you can just drop off the engine at a reputable engine shop and you'll get it back like this, ready to drop in.

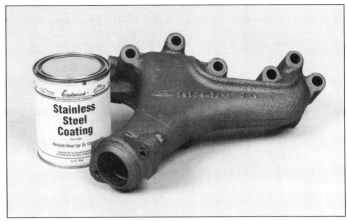

Eastwood's Stainless Steel Coating is excellent for refinishing engine components like exhaust manifolds. Photo courtesy The Eastwood Company.

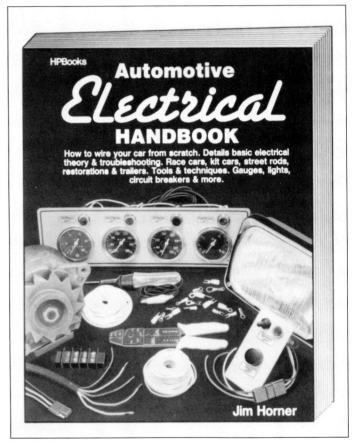

HPBooks' Automotive Electrical Handbook will help take some of the mystery out of your car's electrical system.

Shows & Swap Meets—Part of the fun of restoring an old car is to hunt down those rare and elusive parts. Throughout the year and across the country, major swap meets like Carlisle, Pomona or Pate draw thousands of vendors and tens of thousands of buyers. There are also hundreds of small, local swap meets you can attend. There's no telling where or when that elusive part will turn up, but if you're not looking for it in the right places, you aren't going to find it. Just be careful that you thoroughly check out the parts at a swap meet to make sure they are correct and in good condition.

Clubs—When it comes to parts and information, the best investment you can make is to join a local or national club that specializes in the marque you're interested in. Not only can you get technical support from club experts, there's a good chance that the parts you need are listed for sale in the club newsletter. Furthermore, you can advertise the parts you need in the club newsletter. National clubs also put on an annual meet that comprises a show and swap meet. Not only can you hunt for parts, you can also look over restored versions of your car and talk to the owners. Car collectors are always eager to talk about their restorations and they can answer many of your questions about who supplies parts or performs specialized work.

Junkyards—Back in the early days of the collector car hobby, junkyards were a great place to find parts and accessories. With suburbia spilling out into rural areas where junkyards once thrived, along with environmental regulations and the popularity of crushing old cars for recycling, finding a junkyard with a mother lode of parts is rare today. Out in the hinterlands old-time junkyards still exist, and if you can find one intact, there's good pickings. You may even find a good parts car to cannibalize to complete your restoration.

58

Removing the dashboard completely is the only proper way to go about rewiring your car. Complete, new wiring harnesses are available for many collector cars.

GROUND-UP RESTORATION

By definition, a "ground-up" or "body-off" restoration entails disassembling the entire car, and then repairing and rebuilding each component to like-new condition and reassembling it. Part of a restoration is to utilize as many original components as possible, not only for originality but because these parts are *date-coded*. In a concours restoration, judges will inspect as many components as possible. Alternators, wiper motor covers, steering boxes, exhaust manifolds and rear axles are just some of the parts that are date-coded. If you're doing a concours restoration, it's essential these original parts are rebuilt, restored and installed back on the car.

Methods & Procedures

How you begin your restoration is up to you. If your budget allows you to begin both the mechanical and cosmetic work simultaneously, the restoration will go much faster. If you have to tackle just one area of the car at a time, consider completing the mechanicals first, then body and paint and finally interior.

Some collectors, of course, just have the car dropped off at a restoration shop, and a few months later pick up a completed, restored car. Not all of us can bankroll a restoration like this. Others like getting dirty from time-to-time and have more of an affinity with engines and hard mechanical repair while others are intimidated by engines and stick to trim items and bodywork.

Whatever course you decide there are certain things to keep track of. Organization is the key to restoration. Keeping track of the progress of each area of restoration is important. Ideally, all the different segments—powertrain, chassis and body—are completed at the same time, so the assembly of the car can be handled without interruption.

Engine

Hopefully, the engine is high on your list for rebuilding, however if the miles are low or it has been rebuilt

To get to the transmission on this '37 Packard, the interior needed to be completely disassembled.

previously, you may be able to get by with minor surgery. There's no guarantee the rebuild was done correctly with top-quality parts. You don't want to drive your freshly restored car to a show only to have the engine give up the ghost in the middle of the show field.

Does it Need Rebuilding?—Before removing the engine from the car and disassembling it, first find out what the engine's overall condition is. Are there any unusual noises? Does it smoke? Does it make power? If you aren't mechanically inclined, you can have your mechanic analyze it and give you a report, making sure to indicate that you want a compression check. Low compression is an indication of worn valves and bad piston rings.

Engine noises are obvious signs of trouble. Valvetrain clacking, for example, can indicate rocker arms needing adjustment or defective hydraulic lifters. A heavy thudding or knocking sound can indicate bad main bearings. An engine with valvetrain noises can run for a while but bottom-end noises indicate impending doom. Automotive manuals, such as those from *Motor* and *Chiltons* usually have a section on noise diagnosing, while most of the typical repair manuals you find in stores don't.

Oil burning and low compression are good reasons for rebuilding an engine. With the exception of some major machining operations, this is within the realm of the backyard mechanic—provided you have the necessary tools and literature. HPBooks has several excellent engine rebuild manuals available, as do others that may be found in the Classic Motorbooks catalog. If you do decide on

The suspension is one area you should seriously consider upgrading on your collector car. Polyurethane bushings and gas-pressurized shocks not only promote safety, but offer much better ride quality and handling. Photo by Michael Lutfy.

Eastwood's Chassis Black is extremely durable and protects your suspension components from rust and corrosion. It can only be applied after the part has been completely cleaned, preferably sandblasted. Photo courtesy The Eastwood Company.

an engine rebuild, it might be wise to have hardened exhaust valve seats installed in the cylinder heads. That decision really depends on how you plan on driving your car. If it will see plenty of drag strip action or you'll be towing an Air Stream trailer across the country, then hardened valve seats are highly recommended. For average driving, pre-1972 cars can do just fine running on today's unleaded gas.

Farming Out—It is also well within the capabilities of the restorer to remove the engine from the car, take it apart and then drop it off at the machine shop. Subsidiary components, such as the carburetor, distributor, starter and alternator can be rebuilt and detailed at home. Of course, you can drop these off too and have them rebuilt professionally. Always have the *original* parts rebuilt, if possible, rather than getting replacement parts which may not have the correct, original part numbers and date codes.

Certain parts, such as most modern fuel pumps, for example, may not be readily rebuildable, so you may have to locate an original part in good condition, which may not be an easy task.

Engine Details—Once you have the engine out, you can decide what to do with (assuming your car has them) the air conditioning system, power steering, power brake booster, radiator and any other underhood accessory. If they work fine, perhaps just a thorough cleaning and repaint is all that's required, especially if the part is still in good, serviceable condition. On some components, it doesn't pay to cut corners; it would be wise to have the radiator boiled out, for example, no matter what its condition is.

If you are not doing a complete, body-off restoration, it is considerably easier to restore the engine compartment once the engine is out. It is also that much easier to work

In the interest of safety, you should consider upgrading the braking system as well, especially if your car was originally equipped with front drum brakes. There are front and rear drum brake conversion kits available for many cars. Photo by Michael Lutfy.

Brake lines are commonly overlooked. Replace all rubber lines with new ones. Better yet, invest in stainless steel braided line for maximum durability if originality isn't important. Photo by Michael Lutfy.

This '67 Corvette interior shines as it did the day it rolled off the showroom floor, but only after much hard work. Photo by Michael Lutfy.

Tires are another area that should be upgraded. You should be able to find reproductions of the original tire. Many enthusiasts have one set of modern radials for street driving, and an original set for car shows.

on the front suspension with the engine out of the way, too. Once you get the engine back, spend some time detailing it, especially the areas that will be hard to reach once it is back in the engine compartment. Many auto parts stores carry engine paint.

It's just plain common sense to replace the original hoses, fan belts, and spark plug wires with new ones. Today, correct replacement parts are available for collector cars that duplicate the original codes, markings and colors. If reproductions are not offered, duplicating the makings, codes and colors from the originals can be done.

Chances are, that '67 Corvette interior looked much like this one at first. Reproduction interior kits are available for many collector cars. Check Hemmings for suppliers.

Reupholstering seats does require some special skill and tools. If you're not up to the task, there are plenty of reupholstery shops around. A word of advice is for you to obtain the interior kit yourself, to make sure you get exactly what you want, and hire the shop to install it on the seats.

Eastwood Company offers this Trim Adhesive, which is handy for attaching carpet and vinyl trim to metal. Photo courtesy The Eastwood Co.

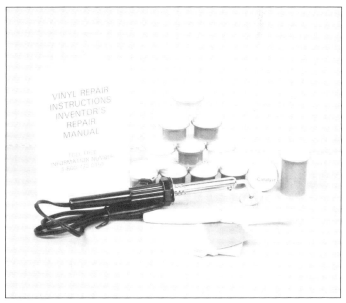

Small rips and tears in vinyl fabric can be repaired using this Vinyl Repair Kit from The Eastwood Company. Photo courtesy The Eastwood Co.

Wiring & Electrical Systems

Some auto enthusiasts have a hard time with the electrical system. It can be hard to understand how electricity works and wiring diagrams aren't that easy to read and decipher. And on those cars that are loaded with electrically operated options, all you have to do is to look underneath the dash to get discouraged. All you'll see are big bundles of different colored wires that are hard to follow and trace.

If your car has electrical problems, you first have to familiarize yourself with the circuit, isolate the problem and then repair the wiring or replace the defective electrical component. This is easier said than done. If you're shaky about electrical circuits, pick up and study a book dealing with automotive electrical systems, such as HPBooks' *Automotive Electrical Handbook*, before you attempt any repairs. Also study the car's wiring diagrams, which may be available from the dealer. Remember that all wires are color-coded and wiring harnesses are like the trunk and branches of a tree. As the harness branches out to the various accessories and circuits, by following

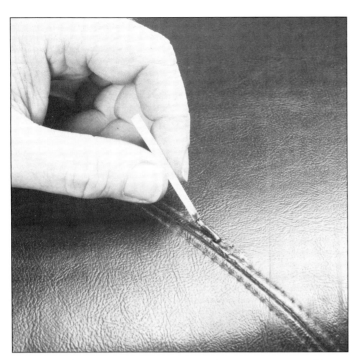

Very small tears in the seat or dashboard can be fused together with Vinyl Fusion, available from Eastwood. Photo courtesy The Eastwood Co.

HPBooks

Paint & Body
HANDBOOK

Straightening steel & aluminum body panels. Gas-welding & art-welding.
Repairing fiberglass. Paint preparation materials, tools & techniques.
Lead vs. plastic filler. Spot repairs & color matching.
Custom paints & techniques.

by Don Taylor & Larry Hofer

Before tackling body and paintwork yourself, read up on the subject.

the color codes it's easier to trace and repair problems than you might think.

The most common problem when repairing electrical wiring is dry-rotted insulation and driveway jury-rigging. This poses a safety hazard and your wiring harness should be repaired. If it's beyond repair, you'll have to replace it. Fortunately, there are a number of companies that sell reproduction wiring harnesses for most American cars. One of the largest is M&H Electric Fabricators (13537 Alondra Blvd., Santa Fe Springs, CA 90670. 213-926-9552).

Steering & Drivetrain

The drivetrain consists of the transmission, driveshaft and rear axle. It is probably more cost- and time-effective to send these components out for repair and/or reconditioning rather than investing in the many specialized tools required for their rebuild.

Transmissions—If your car is equipped with a manual transmission, remember to have the flywheel balanced and turned. Also consider upgrading to one of the newer style clutches now offered by Hayes. If equipped with automatic transmission, be careful that the rebuild shop doesn't replace your unit with a rebuilt transmission. The original transmission is date-coded. You'll lose originality if you settle for a replacement. That replacement M40 for your '69 Camaro may have come from a '72 Firebird.

Rear Axle—For the rear axle, make sure the ring and pinion are inspected for wear and, if it's a limited slip, that the C-clips are in good shape. Have new axle bearings pressed on and request that the rear be set up by an experienced mechanic.

Steering Box—Unless you're an above average mechanic, the same advice applies for steering boxes, both manual and power. However, you should be able to do a good job of detailing them prior to installation. There are a number of reference books that provide detailing information, including *How To Restore Your Musclecar* available from Classic Motorbooks.

Front & Rear Suspension

Suspension work is essentially an R&R (remove and replace) operation, and is well within the reach of the average enthusiast. Some specialized tools are usually required, particularly when it comes to removing ball joints and springs, but these aren't very expensive. *It is*

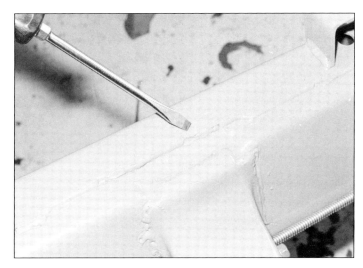

The frame rails on this Corvette were rusted through. As you can see, the seams were repaired with professional welds. This is an example of the type of work you should leave to a professional. Photo by Michael Lutfy.

The rear wheelwells on this LeMans Sport were once cut to accommodate larger tires. This can't be restored without great expense; but it can be replaced with used or reproduction sheet metal.

Body panels are much easier to work on when they are removed. All bodywork must be done in a well-ventilated area, and respirators should be worn. Unlike this fellow, you should also wear goggles or glasses to protect your eyes.

absolutely essential that care be taken when working with coil springs and torsion bars. These components are under tremendous tension and removing them incorrectly can lead to severe personal injury. Therefore, when removing coil springs, *always* use a coil-spring compressor.

Suspension Upgrades—Unless you have a prewar classic, there are many companies offering complete suspension rebuild kits consisting of all the necessary parts needed to revitalize your car's suspension. Here is one area where you may want to upgrade from stock parts if you're not too concerned about originality. Switching from hydraulic to gas-pressurized shocks will improve handling. Polyurethane bushings for control arms and sway bars outlast rubber parts and also improve handling. The improved handling and steering control will give you a much safer and more pleasurable ride.

Brakes—Don't skimp on the braking system. If equipped with drum brakes, make sure the drums are turned and trued. Don't try to reuse old parts—get rid of the old springs and wheel cylinders and replace with all new units. However, if a concours restoration is your goal, you should rebuild the old cylinders since they are date-coded.

If equipped with disc brakes, the same policy applies— get rid of those old parts. Have the rotors turned and calipers inspected. GM four-piston calipers were notorious for leaking. Replacements are now sleeved with

If the body panel can't be repaired or replaced, then a replacement has to be made. This task requires basic metal fabrication skills. HPBooks publishes the Sheet Metal Handbook, the Metal Fabricator's Handbook, and the Welder's Handbook—all offer instruction on how to accomplish this yourself.

stainless steel and are virtually leakproof. Semi-metallic brake pads will improve the braking ability of your car and are a worthwhile, safe investment.

Many novice enthusiasts are confused about the difference between standard brake fluid and silicone fluid. Silicone fluid is an excellent choice if the car is to see limited service, as it tends to resist water better. It is more expensive and remember that standard brake fluid cannot be added to a system filled with silicone fluid.

One other area of the braking system often overlooked is the brake lines. Inspect every inch of the lines for leaking, and replace all rubber lines leading to the wheel cylinders. Inspect the master cylinder and have it rebuilt if necessary. Finally, make sure the parking brake is in good working order and the cables are not frayed or damaged.

Tires—Tires, of course, are part of your car's suspension system. If you are into strict originality, most classic and original type tires are available as reproductions, however, many enthusiasts use modern radials instead. A good idea is to use modern radials for driving because they are safer and improve ride quality and handling, and keep a set of stock original tires to put on for car shows.

Interior, Upholstery & Trim

Here is another area where even the novice can get in and do a good job. Many companies offer the products and kits necessary to make minor repairs. There are also many reproduction interior kits available from various companies that advertise in enthusiast car magazines and *Hemmings,* so you'll be able to replace your interior or restore it to like-new condition.

Carpets—There is nothing like a new set of carpets to rejuvenate an interior. At least, it is a good starting place and fairly easy to replace. Reproduction carpeting is readily available and while you are at it, replace the padding too. If the carpet is fine but just needs a thorough cleaning, there are a variety of cleaners available that will do the job. For more on that, see chapter 5, *Basic Detailing Tips*.

Door Panels & Dash Pads—Door panel replacement is also quite easy. There are a number of companies that offer reproduction door and quarter trim panels. You'll need to transfer any bright moldings and emblems from the old panel to the new, however this is a simple process. Dash pad replacement can be a little more difficult, especially in late Sixties and early Seventies cars. Care must be taken not to damage the pads. Make sure you use plenty of protectorant like *Armor All* or Meguiar's *Intensive Protectant* to soften the pads to avoid cracking.

Seats—When it comes to the reupholstery of your car's seats, you're better off leaving this job to a professional reupholsterer. To save some money, you can locate and obtain the material yourself to avoid any surcharge the reupholsterer my add. Virtually all cars have reproduction upholstery available, and it isn't very expensive. If you haven't had experience recovering seats, you may make a costly mistake. If reproduction upholstery isn't available, you can redye the originals if they are in good shape. The great part about redying is you can assemble pieces from several cars (even if they are different colors) and redye them to look factory-fresh. The same goes for headliners.

Vinyl—Vinyl rips and tears can sometimes be repaired very effectively. If your local reupholstery shop can't or won't repair the rips, contact your local car dealer. You'll find that there are vinyl repairmen who visit dealerships from time to time, repairing rips and tears on trade-ins. Their skill in matching the liquid vinyl color and grain is light years ahead of what an amateur can do. Also, there are several kits available from The Eastwood Co. that will help you repair minor tears yourself.

Instrument Panel—While the interior is apart, disassemble the instrument panel and clean and inspect the instruments. If any of them are not working, there are a number of companies that advertise in *Hemmings* that provide a rebuilding service. Radios can also be serviced, and replacement speakers are available from just about any electronics store that stocks car audio components.

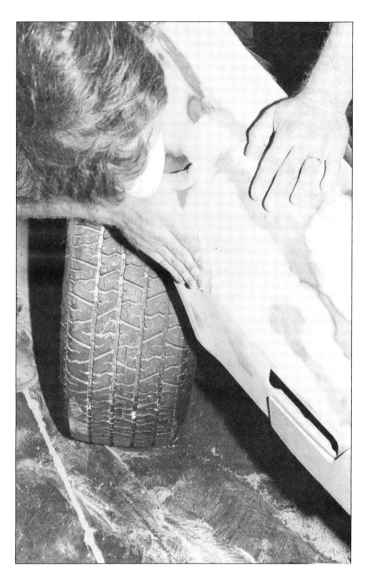

Plastic filler is not a substitute for lead or metal, and should never be used to fill holes in any body panels. It should be used as sparingly as possible (unlike the panel shown here) to fill any low spots in the metal prior to sanding and priming.

Moldings

Chrome-plated trim parts, whether exterior or interior, may have to be removed and sent out for replating. You may be able to find usable replacements at swap meets or as is the case with certain popular cars, reproduced replacement parts are available. Remember that you probably won't be able to match up rechromed and NOS (new-old-stock) pieces. NOS chrome is no match for show chrome, so plan on sending everything out for replating. Anodized trim such as window reveal moldings can be replated. One of the best is Color Brite (2500 Lexington Ave., Kenner, LA 70062. 504-461-8070).

Painted trim and moldings that are worn will need to be repainted. You'll probably end up painting all the

Many people prefer to use two different colors of primer, to help detect any high spots. It is entirely possible for an amateur enthusiast to bring the car's bodywork to this stage prior to painting. By doing the bodywork and primer yourself, you'll save hundreds, if not thousands of dollars.

moldings to insure a correct match because with most cars, the original paint is probably faded. However, be forewarned that it can be difficult to find the correct color codes for interior trim. For example, if you look in the Chrysler parts book, you'll find that all the different trim colors are listed, but there are no codes and the automotive paint shops do not have them either. The only thing to do, at least with a Chrysler car, is to have a paint shop do a color match.

Bodywork & Paint

More than anything else, it is your car's bodywork and paint that will be judged by others. This can mean different things to different people. For someone who is restoring a car with originality as the goal, then any imperfections that the car came with from the factory will be left untouched or will be reproduced when repainted.

Few cars left the assembly plant without some paint runs or overspray. A dedicated restoration will attempt to duplicate these errors.

Others prefer to improve upon what the factory produced and will end up with bodywork and paint that is considerably "better than new." Still, a great paint job seems almost alive—liquid and flowing over every part of the body. However, a great paint job cannot hide any body imperfections, and will in fact draw attention to them.

Paint Removal—Before the painting can be done, the old paint must be removed down to the bare metal. The recommended process is to use a chemical stripper to remove the old paint and primer. Care must be used with chemical strippers. Only work in a well-ventilated area and never use the stripper in direct sunlight. Be prepared to do lots of scraping and scouring to get all the old paint off. Make sure you wear goggles, a mask over your nose and mouth and rubber gloves, as well as clothing to protect your skin. Paint stripper is volatile stuff.

An alternative to stripping is to having the body, frame and other painted parts dipped in a chemical bath. In this process, the entire body is immersed in a large vat filled with chemical removing agents. Redi Strip (main office: 9910 Jordon Circle, Santa Fe Springs, CA 90670 213-944-9915) has 23 facilities across the country that offer chemical dipping. There are pros and cons to dipping. On one hand, it simplifies the paint removal process and certainly will remove all paint and primer, as well as any chemical impurities in the metal. On the other hand, if the chemical agent isn't *completely* removed during the rinse process, it can continue to eat away at the metal, even once the car is painted. There's no guarantee that the agents will entirely be flushed out of the myriad nooks and crevices of a car's body.

Body Inspection—Once the body is down to bare metal, the inspection process begins, and here great attention to detail is an absolute must. Rust is insidious; it can eat away at metal in both exposed and hidden areas. Carefully inspect every inch of the exterior and interior. Climb into the trunk and check the cavities down in the lower quarters. The cowl and the area under the front windshield are very prone to rust. Depending on the rust or collision damage, you may or may not have to replace sheet metal. Fortunately, reproduction sheet metal is offered for many American cars, but here the buyer must be careful about the source. Over the past few years, "offshore" sheet metal, mostly from Asia, has become more popular in the collision repair business, and many reproduction panels are now made of this same type of metal. The problem is the metal is not as pure as quality sheet metal, and because of this, there is acid and other impurities that will actually eat at the metal and bubble under the paint, eventually ruining both.

Used Sheet Metal—One alternative to replacing trunk pans, floor pans, quarter panels and fenders with reproduction or NOS parts is used sheet metal. There are a number of companies that offer sheet metal from the Southwest that is rust-free and quite affordable. These companies advertise in publications such as *Hemmings*.

Preparation—Whether you do it yourself or have the car painted professionally, the key to a good paint job is in the preparation. You'll soon notice the effects of any shortcuts taken after the initial "high" of seeing your car repainted wears off. The preparation of the metal surface is just the first step in a quality paint job. A concern is the use of plastic body filler or "Bondo." Plastic filler is not a substitute for lead or metal. It is instead used to smooth the metal surface prior to sanding and priming. How well the surface is sanded and the first coats of primer are laid down are also important. Many painters prefer to use different colors of primer between coats. For example, by laying down a first coat of red oxide primer followed by gray, when the primer is sanded, the red primer will come through, indicating any high spots that have to be corrected.

Types of Paint—Today's restorer also has to make a choice of what paint to use. If a concours restoration is the goal, then he is obligated to use the same type paint. For example, most American cars of the Fifties, Sixties and Seventies used lacquer (Chrysler used acrylic enamel in the Sixties), so in restoring a car correctly, the paint of choice would be lacquer. There are, however, a variety of other paints now available that look as good as lacquer, are as easy to paint and are far more durable. Another concern is lacquer is slowly being phased out due to pollution considerations. Today, polyurethanes and base coat/clear coat paints are becoming more popular and provide excellent gloss and durability. Talk over with your painter the choices you have and ask for his recommendations. The approach you are taking to the car's identity will play a large part in this decision. If the choice is to go concours, then repaint with the correct type of paint. If you're not a slave to restoration, the sky's the limit.

Applying Paint—When it comes to painting the car yourself, unless you have experience, you may want to pass this job on to a professional. When you get right down to it, painting is an art—with many variables. Having the right equipment is essential. Besides the large amounts of dust and residue that accumulates with the many sanding and resanding steps, paints and solvents are extremely toxic and require a well-ventilated yet sealed work area.

BASIC DETAILING TIPS

5

Even the most mechanically inept enthusiast can detail his car. How much time and effort required depends on the level of perfection you want, and the amount you intend to drive your collector car. Photo by Michael Lutfy.

Most people, at best, wax their daily driver once or twice a year. A collector car deserves much more than such an occasional wash and waxing. As the name implies, *detailing* means cleaning, polishing and waxing all the details. It's painstaking work. Like everything else that is related to collector cars, detailing requires a big initial investment in terms of time and effort, followed by regular maintenance. Detailing is a task in which each piece of metal, glass, rubber and vinyl is cleaned and polished until it gleams. The engine compartment and undercarriage are absolutely sanitary, and the interior sparkles from carpet to headliner. Dirt simply does not exist after a thorough detailing. For many, getting the car to look better than the day it left the dealer is the goal. If you only drive the car occasionally, maintaining that look isn't too difficult once you get to that point.

Detailing also means paying attention to the details of your restoration. This means making sure the correct decals and emblems are in place; that all nuts and bolts are fastened securely, or that the spark plug wires curve properly. In addition to cleaning, detailing includes taking care of all minor imperfections.

Concours Detailing—For those wishing to enter concours type competition, be forewarned. Having a car that is as clean as the day it left the dealership won't cut it in concours competition. Concours cars must be perfect, because the judges will often look for anything wrong. For example, in the judging process, dirt found in the taillight lens housing after the lens was removed is enough for a car to lose points. Spark plug wires that don't curve properly leaving the distributor cap or radiator fins that aren't perfectly straight are reasons for losing points. The time and preparation required for detailing a car for concours competition is enormous. Because concours competition is so keen, 99% of all serious concours cars are no longer driven but must be trailered from show to show.

You'll need a complete supply of high quality car care products, such as the ones shown here.

For some, concours competition epitomizes nitpicking, while to others it is the ultimate form of automotive appreciation.

A typical major detail should be done either immediately after the car is acquired or after any mechanical or cosmetic work is completed. Thereafter, it is just a matter of maintenance. Unless you allow the car to get dirty, there is no reason to do another major detail for at least four months. All that's necessary is to keep after the areas that attract dirt more than others, such as the wheels, wheelwells, grille, engine compartment and undercarriage. The more you drive the car, the more cleaning and maintenance will be required. Remember that concours cars are never driven, so if you drive yours, it will deteriorate, regardless of how well you maintain it.

Detailing doesn't mean just cleaning and polishing; it also means that all of the "details" on your collector car are attended to. This includes making sure all emblems and decals are correct and installed where they should be.

DETAILING SHOPS

No collector in his right mind would take a collectible car to a detailing shop. Detailing shops are geared toward cleaning and refurbishing cars that are to be sold or driven daily. A quality restoration shop, however, will do a thorough job on all facets of a collector car, leaving no stone unturned in the quest for cleanliness. Remember that it's easy to maintain a restored car that isn't driven. A driver can be detailed, but never to concours specifications. However, a detailing shop can do a stand-up job on a driver that will turn heads on the street. They can charge as much as several hundred dollars and even take several days, and although the results can be excellent, there are still areas that they've probably missed. It all depends on what you want them to do. Detail shops try and give you the best, most noticeable results for the money. For example, while you can spend an entire day cleaning and dressing the interior of your car, or even also spend an entire day on just the wheels, the typical detail shop won't. They will do a decent job but to get the interior or wheels absolutely perfect may require many, many hours of labor. Detailing also includes things such as the wheelwells and the underbody. Each customer's demand will be different. One person may be happy with a beautiful interior, exterior and engine but may not want to go beyond that. You have to specify exactly what you want and be willing to pay the bill for labor and time invested by the detailer.

EXTERIOR DETAILING

Of course, you probably fall into the category of a "serious collector," and if you're short on mechanical skills, this is an area where you can derive hours of enjoyment by honing the appearance of the car yourself. All you need is the time, the right materials and a lot of "elbow grease."

Assuming you're starting with a dirty, street-driven car, your first step should be to coat the lower body sides, wheelwells, and wheels with kerosene. Kerosene won't hurt the paint, but it will dissolve any road grime, dirt, tar and the like. If one application doesn't do the trick, try as many as it takes. If your car is undercoated, kerosene will loosen it up and dissolve it, so be careful. Use plenty of water to rinse the kerosene off. If there are any particularly stubborn spots, use a bug and tar

remover, which contains stronger dissolving agents with kerosene being the prime ingredient in most of them.

Washing

You'll find that many detailing manuals recommend using a dish detergent to wash your car. Dish detergents are fine as long as you understand they will strip away any wax or polish on the finish. If you're starting with a dirty car that has road tar and oxidized paint, dish detergent will work well. Once the car has been cleaned and waxed, use one of the many detergents designed to remove dirt but leave the wax finish, like Meguiar's *Hi-Tech Wash* or *Zip Wax* car wash or a similar product from a car care manufacturer.

Washing Procedures—Hose the car down from top to bottom, loosening surface dirt which can scratch paint. To avoid scratching the paint, use a soft cotton terry cloth wash mitt, which does not absorb dirt particles that will damage the paint finish. Don't use the typical household sponge, because it can trap and hold dirt. The resulting

For serious detailing, you'll need to get into all nooks and crannies, and a set of professional brushes like these from Turtle Wax will make the job easier.

Never wash the car in direct sunlight. Dish detergents are fine, as long as you realize they will strip any wax. For best results, use a soft cotton terry cloth wash mitt.

scratches may be small, but cumulatively, they will dull the paint. Also, it's important to constantly rinse the car and to empty the bucket or wash pail several times and refill with fresh detergent and clean water.

Never wash or wax a car in the direct sun; water evaporates and leaves water spots. Wash in the shade or during late evening or early morning when the sun is not as strong. Never try to wax a car when the temperature falls below 50 degrees Fahrenheit. When drying, use a quality chamois cloth, followed by a soft Turkish towel.

Paint Chips

At this stage, you may want to take care of any paint chips with a small touch-up paint kit. If none is available for your car, an automotive paint store should be able to mix some up for you. Automotive paint stores should have the color code listing for your car. If they don't, you can find the color codes listed on the data plate attached to the firewall or cowl, or check with the car dealer or with a car club. If absolutely nothing is available, drive the car to the paint store or remove a painted part and take it to the store and ask them to match it.

Touch-up Procedures—Make sure all wax and polish has been removed from the area to be touched up. Using a fine brush, build successive layers of paint on the chip until the painted area is a little higher than the surrounding paint. Let it dry for about a week. Then sand the paint down with #600 or finer wet sandpaper until the painted area is the same level as the rest of the paint. Follow up with several applications of sealer and glaze

To wash dirt out of small crevices around emblems and grille work, you'll need a small brush such as this one made with horsehair from Eastwood. Photo courtesy The Eastwood Company.

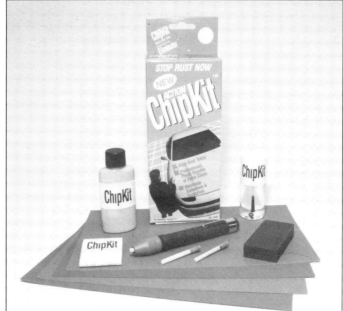

The Action ChipKit from Pro Motorcar products enables car owners to fix paint chips and scratches, particularly those irritating door dings you pick up in parking lots. The kit includes the Eliminator glass-fiber brush to remove surface rust, grime and wax around the chip; paint sealer, fine sanding papers and block and an extra fine polishing compound. For more information, or to obtain a kit, contact: Pro Motorcar Products, 22025 U.S. 19 N., Clearwater, FL 34625. 800/323-1090.

and wait at least a month for the paint to cure before you wax the affected area.

Waking Up Sleeping Paint

When the exterior is clean you'll be able to see what condition the paint is in. If your car's paint looks dull and doesn't have much shine, that indicates the top layer of paint has oxidized. There is nothing you can do to bring that layer of paint back; all you can do is remove it, exposing the healthy paint below. By removing the dead top layer, you'll also remove light scratches, water spots and swirl marks. The trick here is knowing how much paint to remove and what materials to use. Thereafter, wax is used to inhibit further oxidation while allowing the paint to breath.

Finish Restorers—If the paint surface is in good condition, all you may need is a finish restorer. Most of these, like Turtle Wax's *Color Back*, come in liquid form, which makes them easy to apply. Stronger than a wax or polish but not as strong as rubbing compound, finish restorers remove very light oxidation, grime, tar and light swirl marks. However, they generally don't offer much in the

way of wax protection. Meguiar's *Car Cleaner Wax* has three cleaners; fine-cut, medium-cut and heavy-cut cleaners that safely remove surface defects. Which one you choose depends on the severity of the defects. After that, a thorough waxing is in order.

You may get away with using a sealer and glaze on moderately oxidized paint. The fine grit in the polish removes surface imperfections. After using one of these products, follow up with a good carnauba waxing.

Rubbing Compounds—Unless the paint surface is severely oxidized and has deep scratches, avoid using rubbing compounds. The danger here is, because of the abrasives contained, you can go down to the primer—necessitating new paint. Use rubbing compounds only as a last resort. If you can't save the paint by compounding, a paint job is unavoidable.

Waxing & Polishing

The terms "waxing" and "polishing" today are interchangeable. When using waxes, make sure the product is compatible with the condition of your car's surface. Unless specified, all waxes contain a mild abrasive to

If the paint is lightly oxidized and has fine scratches, a product like Safe Cut from The Wax Shop will remove the top layer of dead paint. Then you can apply a wax to protect the new layer.

Meguiar's Vibrant Paint Shield is a one-step finish restorer that cleans, polishes and protects. It has non-abrasive cleaners that remove minor paint imperfections without scratching or swirling, and it safely eliminates harmful environmental contaminants that can dull all paint finishes.

remove surface oxidation. Unless your paint surface is brand new or nearly new, these products are fine. If, however the paint is new or nearly new, use a non-abrasive wax, such as Turtle Wax's *Non-Abrasive* car wax on new paint.

Generally, products that contain carnauba wax are preferred, mainly because carnauba is the most durable. Stay away from waxes or polishes that contain silicone; their chemical bonding with the paint will make paint touch-up nearly impossible. And don't fall for the claim that you only have to wax your car once a year. A good carnauba wax will protect a daily-driven car about 3-4 months.

How often should you wax? It all depends on weather conditions and how the wax is holding up. If water still beads then there is still wax on the paint. You should wax your car at least four times a year and use a cleaner wax at least once a year to remove old wax buildup. Some enthusiasts wax every month; there is a noticeable difference in doing so, because the paint just shines better. **Waxing Procedure**—How you apply the wax or pol-

ish can make a big difference in the final product. Some waxes come with a small applicator pad—don't use it because it will grab and hold any grit or dirt that was left behind by any polishing operations. This is especially true if you've previously used a rubbing compound which contains abrasive particles. Instead, use soft cotton diapers or plenty of soft cotton towels. Don't crumple it up in a wad; a crumpled up wad will have sections that don't have any wax on them which can scratch the paint. Also remove any rings or other jewelry and take care not to get too close to the car with belt-buckles or zippers.

Wrap the towel around two fingers, apply some wax on it and work it into a small area. It is best to wax then buff one small area at a time. Always apply the wax on the cloth and not on the paint and always use the minimum amount that is necessary, using a tight, circular motion.

Heavy applications of wax will leave streaks and will clog your towel. Once saturated with wax residue, the towel won't buff properly, and a heavy coat is much harder to buff off. If you feel you need a heavy coat of wax,

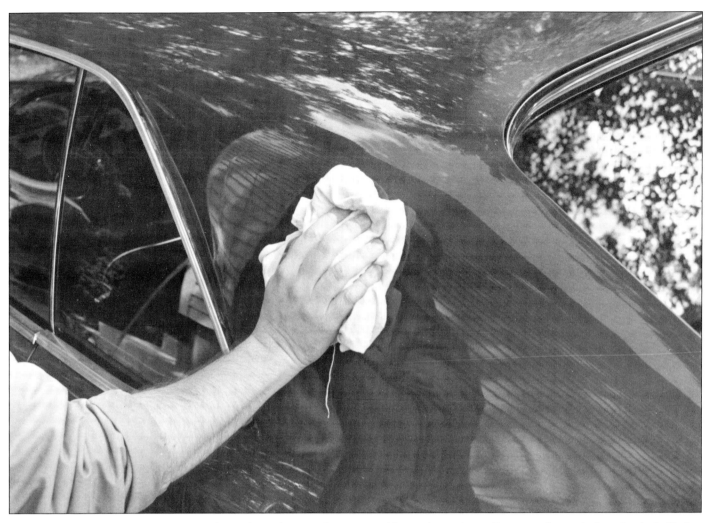

Don't bunch up the towel or diaper as you apply wax. Instead, use two fingers around the towel to apply wax. Do one small area at a time, then buff off before moving to another area.

it is best to apply two light coats instead of just one heavy one. Just use a sparring amount, rub it in well, reducing pressure as the wax begins to dry. If this is done correctly, the dried wax will hardly be noticeable and the residue will easily come off when you buff it out.

Too much wax will also dry in any cracks and crevices and you'll have to take extra time to get it out later. A soft detailing brush or a toothbrush will remove wax from crevices. After the wax has dried, use fresh, clean cloths or cotton towels to buff the finish to a fine luster.

After waxing, you can wipe down the car with a damp cotton terry cloth towel to remove any accumulated dust or a soft brush like the *Car Duster*.

Buffers—A word on buffers. Using a buffer will speed up any polishing process, however you can very easily ruin an otherwise good paint job because you can "burn" the paint and remove it by pressing down too hard. Use a buffer with slow rpms and don't put any pressure on the buffer—let the buffer do the work. Gently glide the buffer slowly along the paint surface, and don't linger on sharp corners or curves.

Sandpaper—Regarding sandpaper, some people will use a very fine wet/dry sandpaper to smooth the paint and to remove orange peel and other surface imperfections. Sanding takes a lot of paint off—it is easy to get to the primer. If the paint is badly oxidized, use polishing compound to remove the top layer. Remember that even rubbing compound won't restore dead paint.

Other Exterior Details

Windows—Just as important as shiny paint is having clean windows. Veteran concours participants use water mixed with a little ammonia and newspapers to clean window glass. It isn't the paper itself that polishes, but

Wax will build up in small cracks and crevices, such as in areas like this door handle. A small, soft-haired brush should be used to remove wax from these areas.

If you garage your car and don't drive it in foul weather very often, you only need to wax it about four or five times a year. In between wax jobs, you can use Meguiar's Quik Detailer, a wipe on/wipe off product that enhances a car's deep shine and protection. It's especially useful if you've been caught in a sudden rainstorm, or have been the unlucky target of tree sap or bird droppings.

rather the ink which acts as a fine abrasive. After cleaning, use a product like *Windex* as a polish.

For plastic rear windows on convertibles, Meguiar's offers a 2-step plastic window polish and cleaner that removes fogging and scratches and restores plastic windows to like-new condition.

For windshields that are scratched or pitted there are glass polishing kits available from The Eastwood Company. These kits contain special glass polishing compounds and a polishing wheel, which can be used with a standard drill to remove light scratches, wiper haze and sand sparkle.

Chrome—Chrome and bright trim can be polished and waxed. You may want to replace severely pitted trim and emblems with new ones as they will be a blemish on an otherwise cleanly detailed car. Painted emblems should also be touched up.

Rubber & Vinyl—Rubber and vinyl should first be thoroughly cleaned. *Murphy's Oil Soap* is very good for this. You may want to repeat the cleaning process on these because they tend to hold dirt. After they are dry, spray with *Armor All*, STP *Son of a Gun* or Meguiar's *Intensive Protectant*, letting it soak in. Follow the instructions on the product—*Armor All* is water based; applying it and not buffing off the excess can do more harm than good. Putting more on isn't going to make it glossier. If the glossy look turns you off, then give Meguiar's *Intensive Protectant* a try. It offers similar reconditioning and protectant qualities without leaving a shiny finish.

Vinyl and convertible tops require extra effort. Vinyl tops are very porous and are prone to trapping dirt. Start by using dish detergent and apply with a brush or you can use a vinyl top cleaner such as Turtle Wax *Vinyl Top Cleaner*. Stubborn cases may require the use of a cleanser such as *Soft Scrub*. A vinyl top dressing must be used after the cleaning process to protect it, otherwise the vinyl will fade. However, don't use a protectorant like *Armor All*; the top will be "patchy" with some areas flat and others glossy. Get a special vinyl conditioner made for vinyl tops.

On the other hand, if the vinyl is already severely faded, it may be more cost- and time-effective to have a new vinyl or convertible top installed. It will be brand-new and much easier to maintain. You can also find out if there is any rust damage underneath a vinyl top.

A mirror-like finish, such as the one on this Boss 429 Mustang, should be what you're striving for. Photo by Michael Lutfy.

If the plastic window on your convertible top is fogged and scratched, try Meguiar's plastic window cleaner and polish formulas before you replace them. Photo by Michael Lutfy.

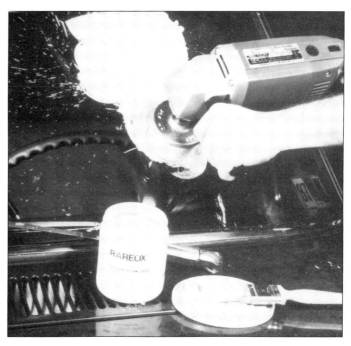

Eastwood's Glass Polishing Kit includes everything except for a hand drill to remove light scratches and pits from your windshield. Photo courtesy The Eastwood Company.

Chrome moldings may need replating or replacing to get them to this condition. Vinyl roofs should be scrubbed with a vinyl cleaner, not dish detergent. After it is clean, use a specially made vinyl top conditioner, not a protectorant like Armor All. Most protectorants don't adhere evenly on vinyl tops.

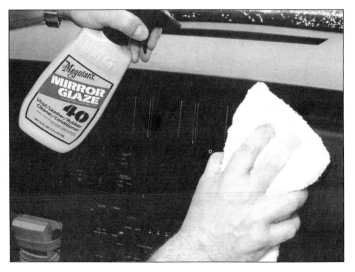

Interior materials need special cleansers and protectorants. There are plenty available. Photo by Michael Lutfy.

WHEELS & TIRES

It has been said that wheels and tires can make or break a car. They have to be as clean and detailed as everything else. In fact, a nice set of wheels and tires on a so-so car can bring the car "up" more than anything else. Wheels and tires are also one of the harder areas to keep clean.

Detailing Wheels

The best way to clean the wheels is to remove them from the car. Start by using dish detergent and warm water on the wheels and tires. Stubborn deposits may require the use of a chemical wheel cleaner such as those made by Eagle One or Mother's. Use a stiff nylon bristle brush to scrub the tire sidewall and tread.

Few items are handier than Eastwood's Water-Jet Wheel Brush when it comes to cleaning wheels and other tricky areas such as grilles. It attaches to a regular garden hose. After washing, the wheels should be painted or polished. New lug nuts should be installed as well. Photo courtesy The Eastwood Company.

Painted wheels can be cleaned and repainted. Always use enamel paint on wheels because it is stronger than lacquer and won't require any buffing. Another popular, although expensive method is to have the wheels powder-coated, where the paint is "baked" onto the wheel. Metal hubcaps should be cleaned and polished (and sometimes painted) like any other brightwork.

Finally, if your car has styled steel factory or aluminum wheels, invest in a new set of chrome lug nuts, center caps and trim rings if the existing ones are damaged, pitted or rusted. Small "details" like these can be the difference between winning first and second place.

Tires can be revitalized with specially made tire cleaners such as those from Eagle One or Meguiar's. Westley's *Bleche-Wite* will clean the lettering on the tires superbly.

Wheelwells should be flushed out and washed with kerosene. Ideally, you'll have done major repair and painting during the restoration process. Thereafter, a thorough cleaning should keep them looking new. How often depends on how much you drive your car.

Detailing Tires

Whitewalls and raised white letters can be rejuvenated by a whitewall cleaner, such as Westley's *Bleche-Wite*. Follow directions closely, and don't allow any of the cleaner to dry on any wheel surfaces as they may stain them. The rest of the tire should then be cleaned and soaked with a protectant, such as *Armor All*, or Eagle One's *Tire Cleaner* for several hours. If you don't like the glossy, freshly dressed look, wash the tires with mild soap and water, and coat the tires with Meguiar's *Intensive Protectant*. Be forewarned that *Armor All* and other protectorants will not last long in rain and require frequent applications to maintain the new tire look.

UNDERBODY

Unless you are doing a ground-up restoration, you can only do so much when it comes to the underbody of your car. Some areas are easy to get to, such as wheelwells. To get these clean, remove the wheels and flush the wheelwells with a hose forcing out as much dirt as possible. After they are dry, you can decide whether you want to repaint the area or undercoat it. You may also find it necessary to remove any wheelwell moldings in order to remove dirt. Use brushes to remove heavily caked-on dirt and also use lots of dish detergent and water to get the area as clean as possible. If you have access to compressed air, use it to force dirt and water out of chassis drain holes.

Undercoating—If your car has been undercoated, you have two choices. You can flush the underbody area, get it as clean as possible and apply a fresh coat; or you can remove the undercoating with kerosene. It's a dirty, time-consuming job that will require hours on your back. If you take this route, wear old clothes and eye protection, because dirt and undercoating will rain down on you.

To do a proper underbody job, the rear axle, springs, shocks, gas tank and exhaust system should be removed and detailed separately. On cars which have a separate body and chassis, such as Corvettes, the body can be lifted off to expose these components. With unibody construction, there is no separate chassis and the suspension components are bolted on directly to the body structure or subframe, so they can be removed separately. Obviously, detailing the underbody is much easier if done during the restoration.

Show cars, such as this hand-built street rod, have no limits when it comes to detailing, even in the suspension. Photo by Michael Lutfy.

INTERIOR

It will be a lot easier to clean and detail the interior if you remove the seats. This may not be as hard as it seems. On some cars, it is simply a matter of loosening a few nuts and then sliding the seat out. On other cars, the nuts may be accessible from the bottom of the car.

Carpet

At this point, it is a good idea to remove the floor *scuff plates*, which usually hold the carpets down, so you can take a look underneath the carpets. Any moisture underneath the carpets is a bad sign. Check for any rust and any water leaks. If the carpets are borderline acceptable, this is a good time to replace them. Also inspect the carpeting up under the foot wells for signs of water stains from a leaking windshield.

Cleaning—If the carpets are stained and dirty but not worn, the first step in rejuvenating their looks is to thoroughly vacuum to remove all loose dirt. Now use a heavy-duty carpet shampoo to clean the carpets. Never shampoo the carpets outside of the car, as they can shrink and won't fit when reinstalled. If the lower door panels are also covered with carpeting, shampoo them as well. Don't use too much water, just enough to keep the shampoo wet. Allow it to dry and then vacuum thoroughly once again.

Cloth, Leather & Vinyl—To clean cloth and vinyl, start from the back and work your way forward, using an upholstery cleaner to clean any cloth-covered areas, including the headliner. A cloth headliner is like a sponge when it comes to smoke and several applications may be required to remove stains and odors. In fact, cleaning an interior that was the home of a heavy smoker requires

Here's an example of a near flawless interior. Note how all interior trim shines. Photo courtesy Musclecar Review.

extra effort as the smoke permeates everything. Work carefully as you clean the headliner; on older cars the fabric can weaken and tear if scrubbed too hard.

Vinyl-covered interior surfaces and seats can be cleaned with dish detergent and water (used sparingly) or you can use one of the many vinyl cleaners offered such as Turtle Wax *Vinyl-Fabric Upholstery* cleaner and protectant. Don't use soap and water or any other cleaner on leather; try a damp cloth first. On really dirty leather, use Lexol-pH *Leather Cleaner*, followed by Lexol *Leather Conditioner and Preservative*. Meguiar's *Medallian for All Leather*, is also excellent.

Dash Panel

On the dash panel, first remove all knobs. You may also want to remove the radio and any other subassembly just to make it easier to clean them. On metal dashes, use a sealer and glaze. Badly scratched metal will require reconditioning and repainting. Vinyl-covered dashes can be cleaned as described earlier. If the plastic instrument lenses are lightly scratched, use Meguiar's two-step plastic polish to remove scratches. If the lenses are badly clouded or scratched, replace them with new units. Many times, you'll find that painted interior parts, such as knobs, levers and the like, will show so much wear that

there is no more paint on them, exposing bare plastic or metal. In this case, you may be better off repainting, replating or replacing them all in order to maintain a uniform match.

After cleaning, all vinyl and plastic trim should be sprayed with *Armor All* or Meguiar's *Intensive Protectant*. Remember that protectants like *Armor All* are water-based, so make sure you buff off all excess. Metal and plated interior trim should be polished and waxed; badly pitted trim should be sent out for rechroming. If you decide to rechrome the interior trim, remove and send all of it out for replating at one time in order to maintain a uniform look. You'll find that most rechroming services advertise in *Hemmings Motor News*.

Trunk

One of the most overlooked areas is the trunk. After a thorough cleaning you'll know if it needs to repainted. Many trunks are sprayed with a spatter-type paint while others are painted body color. If equipped with a rubber trunk floor mat, there may be surface rust under the mat that will have to be removed. Check for water stains or flakes of rust that are tip-offs to a leaking rear window. Depending on condition, you may also have to replace any trunk mats. On some cars, such as 1965-70

Don't forget to detail door panels and all attaching hardware and trim. Replacement panels are easily located at parts reproduction houses that specialize in your make.

For deep cleaning and conditioning of leather interior surfaces, Lexol products are highly recommended by professional detailers. Photo courtesy The Eastwood Company.

Mustangs, the trunk floor is formed by the top of the gas tank. It may be easier to remove the tank to get to any hidden dirt or rust trapped where the tank meets the body.

Paint and detail the jack assembly. Clean and detail the spare and if damaged, make sure the jacking instructions label is replaced with a correct reproduction. Check the rear lamp harness for splices or frayed wiring.

ENGINE COMPARTMENT

With many cars it is the engine itself that makes the car unique, such as 426 Hemi-powered Chryslers and Boss 429 Mustangs. With special cars like these, much of a full-blown restoration will be spent detailing the engine and engine compartment for correctness.

Cleaning—If you don't plan on pulling the car apart but want to detail the engine and engine compartment, you can still do a reasonably good job. The first step is to clean the engine compartment. One of the best places to clean your engine is at the do-it-yourself hand car wash with pressurized hoses. Make sure the engine is fully warmed up, and seal the distributor and carburetor to prevent any water from making the engine difficult to restart later. Use a spray degreaser, such as *Gunk*, and spray liberally on the engine and the engine compartment, taking care not to spray on the exterior paint. You'll want to scrape off any heavy deposits of grease and grime. Let the degreaser work for several minutes and then hit it with the pressure wash. Depending on how dirty the engine is, you may have to repeat this process several times. Be prepared to have to dry out the inside of the distributor cap to get the car started again. You'll be surprised how clean the engine and engine compartment will be after several applications.

Any component that can be removed and detailed outside the engine compartment will be easier to clean and at the same time, expose previously hard-to-reach areas. For example, removal of the alternator, power steering pump, fan and pulleys makes them easier to clean and

Metal dash panels need to be detailed like the car's exterior sheet metal. Sometimes they are painted body color with the same style paint. Waxing and buffing with quality products are what brings out the shine here. Photo by Michael Lutfy.

paint and allows you to access those areas of the engine hidden by these components. Removing the radiator makes the front of the engine more accessible as well, plus the radiator must be cleaned, the fins straightened and the assembly repainted. Remove the battery tray, and if heavily corroded, replace with a new one. Clean the battery and dress the terminals. Clean the cables and inspect for wear. Older cars used spring-type clamps. These are available from several reproduction sources that advertise in *Hemmings Motor News*.

Painting—Of course, painting the engine and engine compartment while it is in the car is difficult at best. If your engine's paint is basically ok, you can just touch up damaged areas. Use a small brush to get hard-to-reach spots. Remove any overspray with lacquer thinner.

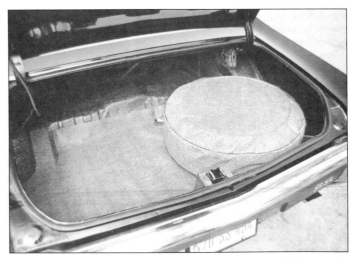

Don't forget the trunk, because you can be sure the judges won't! Many trunks, such as the one in this SS454, are repainted with spatter paint, used originally in many domestic cars in the Sixties and Seventies. This is a fine job.

With many collector cars, it is the engine that makes it unique. Such is the case with the ultra-rare Boss 429 Mustang. Extra care should be taken to detail the car's strongest asset. Photo by Michael Lutfy.

Cables & Hoses—If the degreaser didn't remove all the grease on wiring harnesses, use lacquer thinner to clean them. This is a good time to inspect the harnesses for frayed wires and damaged wrapping. Most car makers used PVC tape to wrap harnesses. You can get this tape at any hardware or electrical supply store. Unwrap the harness, repair any damaged wires and then rewrap the harness. Spark plug wires and the distributor cap should be removed and checked. If necessary, replace them with either reproductions or correct service replacement units. The same goes for the upper and lower radiator hoses and the heater hoses. If they are soft, replace them with either reproductions or correct service replacements. Never use flexible radiator hoses, only correctly molded upper and lower radiator hoses. Also inspect the belts for wear and replace as necessary.

The Grime Blaster from Eastwood attaches to a compressor to pressure-clean your engine compartment with solvent. Photo courtesy The Eastwood Co.

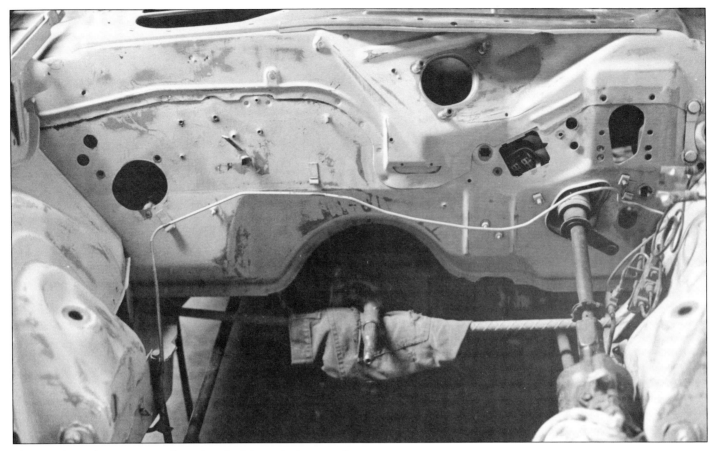
Cleaning the engine compartment is much easier if the engine is removed.

At this point you also have to decide how you want the engine to look after it is detailed. Some want to preserve factory check marks, stickers and stampings and the like as a measure of originality. Make notes of specific marking and codes, and reproduce these once the engine is painted. Also replace any original stickers and decals with reproductions. While refurbishing your engine in this fashion won't be good enough for a concours show, you'll be surprised how well your car can do at smaller, local shows where point judging is not done and absolute cleanliness and correctness is not as critical.

Make sure the inner fenders and firewall are finished correctly. Bare metal parts can be polished while painted surfaces should be waxed with a one step cleaner and wax.

Hood—Finally, give some attention to the underside of the hood. Some cars have a hood pad designed to absorb noise and heat but which also absorbs dirt. It may not be possible to clean it without ruining it. Reproduction hood pads and pad clips are available for many cars. If a reproduction is not offered and you can not find a pad similar to yours that you can cut to fit, then refinish the underside of the hood in body color or semi-gloss black, whichever is correct for your car.

This Boss 429 engine is clean, but not very well detailed. Not how deteriorated the sticker is on the valve cover, and the chips on the block that indicate the need for painting. Photo by Michael Lutfy.

On the other hand, this Boss 429 has had just about every component professionally polished. Photo by Michael Lutfy.

MAINTAINING A COLLECTOR CAR

6

After all the hard work and expense that went into your restoration, it only makes sense to maintain your collector car by servicing it regularly, and storing it properly. A car cover is a must. Photo courtesy The Eastwood Company.

A restored car requires just as much maintenance as a daily driven vehicle. How it is maintained when it's not driven is just as important as when it is on the road. Protecting the finish with wax is just the first step. Simple, preventative maintenance on your car's drivetrain should also be rigorously followed. It's really only a matter of protecting your investment.

Oil Changes

As it is for your daily-driven car, oil changes are important for a collectible car. Many collector cars aren't driven much but still require an oil change at regular intervals—2,000-3,000 miles or, at the very least, twice a year. This is necessary because when oil is exposed to air it will begin to *oxidize*.

Synthetic Oil—Even if the car isn't driven often, you may want to consider a synthetic oil, such as *Mobil 1*, *Redline* or *Amsoil*. Synthetic oil offers several advantages.

For example, unlike conventional motor oils, synthetics can withstand considerably higher temperatures, to the order of 700 degrees as opposed to 300-350 degrees for petroleum-based lubricants. This is important, because the upper cylinder areas of an engine will see temperatures in the 600-degree range. A conventional oil will begin to break down and oxidize almost immediately. Oxidation occurs when the hot oil is exposed to the air which then leads to the formation of organic acids that combine and form varnish deposits, tar and sludge. That is why frequent changes are recommended with conventional oils, while synthetics, because they don't break down as quickly, can go much longer between changes.

In addition, synthetics have much higher film strength, which results in much less blow-by past the piston rings—again reducing oil contamination. Synthetics also lower temperatures in the crankcase and because they are "slipperier," mileage improves. An important benefit for

91

Coolant should be replaced every two years regardless of how often you drive your car. Be sure to use a 50/50 ratio of coolant to water for best results. Also, frequently check all other areas of the cooling system, such as belts, hoses, clamps and the radiator cap.

You may want to consider using a synthetic engine oil for several reasons. Synthetics can withstand nearly twice the oil temperature as regular oil, and have higher lubricating properties.

the collector car that isn't driven as often is synthetics also have the distinct advantage of having an affinity to metal. They adhere to internal metal engine parts, unlike conventional oils that drain off very quickly. If the car sits for extended periods of time, a synthetic provides considerably more protection and prevents damage from so-called "dry" starts.

Drain Plugs—Another wise addition is a magnetic drain plug in the oil pan, replacing the original plug. This is an inexpensive modification that prevents small metal particles from circulating in the oil by clinging to the magnetic plug. When the plug is removed to drain the oil, simply clean the metal particles from the plug and reinstall once the pan is drained.

Manual transmission and rear axle fluids should be changed during the time of restoration. Thereafter, they really won't need to be changed until after 75,000 miles or so, unless you're going to be towing with or racing your collector car. But for normal use, and because you'll likely be limited to 2500 miles per year of driving due to insurance restrictions, you probably won't need to change it again. Photo by Michael Lutfy.

Coolant

The coolant in your radiator should be changed at least every two years with a 50-50 ratio of water to anti-freeze; putting in any more anti-freeze is not recommended. Although anti-freeze raises the boiling point of water by 15 degrees (with a 15-lb. pressure cap) as well as protecting against freezing, anti-freeze inhibits heat absorption and slows the rate by which the water/anti-freeze mixture releases heat.

When changing the anti-freeze, make sure that the rest of the cooling system is in good condition. Check all the hoses, clamps and radiator cap. Soft hoses should be replaced. When flushing the cooling system, use a reverse-flow flushing kit (such as the one offered by Prestone). Reversing the flow of water through the various passages of the cooling system will remove scale and rust that may not be removed by flushing in only one direction. Once the system is flushed, remove the heater hose with the reverse-flow valve and install a new heater hose. Keep the old hose for the next time you flush the system.

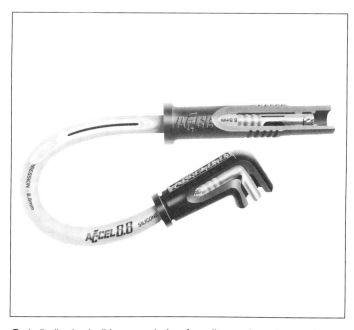

Periodically check all hoses and wires for splits, cracks and general wear. Spark plug wires should definitely be routed away from high temperature areas like exhaust manifolds. If a spark plug wire is burned or split, replace the entire set. If originality isn't important, high-quality, performance wires such as those from Accel are recommended.

93

You should perform a major tune-up every two years or 24,000 miles with most carbureted, non-computerized engines with point-type distributors, with minor tune-ups at six month intervals. Part of a major tune-up includes setting the carburetor's idle speed, fuel mixture and choke.

Other Fluid Levels

The fluids used in the power steering pump, automatic transmission, manual transmission and rear axle should all be changed when you first get your car or during the restoration. Again, synthetic fluids are available for all these applications and are recommended. Check these fluid levels each time the car is to be driven, at each oil change or at least every six months.

Manual Transmission—Manual transmission and rear axle fluids don't have to changed often. Every 75,000-100,000 miles is an acceptable interval because these heavy oils deteriorate very slowly. The only time you would want to change them more often is if the car is used for "heavy service" such as racing or trailer towing. Check their level every six months.

Automatic Transmission—If the car is equipped with an automatic transmission, change the fluid every 15,000 miles and the filter every 30,000 miles. If, during the course of driving, the car overheats, check the transmission fluid immediately. Most automatic transmission oil coolers are routed through the lower radiator tank; if the engine has overheated, it's possible the automatic transmission fluid also overheated which will lead to transmission failure.

TUNE-UPS

Unless the engine is rebuilt when the car is restored, perform a major tune-up before you begin driving the car—it's much easier to follow a maintenance schedule thereafter because you are starting with a freshly tuned engine.

The ground-pounding 426 Hemi is notoriously difficult to keep in a constant state of tune. Frequent engine maintenance is required for engines like these for maximum performance.

Major Tune-ups—A major tune-up includes new spark plugs, points, condenser (if so equipped), distributor cap, rotor and spark plug wires. Change the oil, oil filter, air filter, fuel filter, PCV valve and hose and all vacuum hoses. Set the timing, adjust the carburetor's idle speed, fuel mixture and choke and lubricate all the throttle and carburetor linkages. If equipped with emissions equipment (EGR, air pump, etc.), make sure these are in good working order. Adjust the valve lash on engines equipped with solid lifter camshafts according to settings found generally in a *Chilton's* or *Haynes* engine manual. Finally, adjust the clutch or check the vacuum lines to the automatic transmission.

Minor Tune-up—Every six months afterwards, a minor tune-up will be necessary. A minor tune-up involves checking the timing, the carburetor and inspecting the filters and topping off all the fluid levels.

Frequency—A major tune-up should be performed every two years/24,000 miles thereafter; a minor tune-up every six months. It may not be necessary to change all the components specified above, especially if you only drive the car 2,000-3,000 miles per year, but they should be inspected at regular intervals to keep the engine running at peak performance.

Certain high-horsepower musclecar era engines, such as the 426 Chrysler Hemi, came with two carburetors and a solid lifter camshaft. The Hemi is known for its ability to frequently go out of tune. These engines require constant tuning for optimum performance.

Don't overlook the air filter. Change it frequently, preferably with a high-quality unit like a K&N. After changing the filter, don't forget to replace the rubber seal ring around the carburetor and reconnect all hoses. Photo by Michael Lutfy.

It's a good idea to have a professional, reputable mechanic check out your car with diagnostic equipment as part of the major tune-up.

Other Underhood Maintenance

All accessory drive belts should be checked at every oil change for correct belt tension. This information can be found in the factory service manual or *Chilton's* repair manual. Inspect the underside of the belts for any fraying and cracking, and replace any that look suspect.

Battery—Unless it's a maintenance-free battery, check each cell for proper electrolytic levels and fill with dis-tilled water only. Make sure the battery cables are routed away from the exhaust manifolds and use a battery brush tool to clean the terminals and clamps at least once a year.

Miscellaneous Bolts—Tighten down the valve cover bolts, timing cover bolts and oil pan bolts once a year. These have a habit of loosening up, resulting in oil leaks. If so equipped, have the air conditioning system checked out professionally and recharged once a year.

Brake Fluid—Check the brake master cylinder fluid level at every oil change and every time your car is tuned-up. It is normal for cars with disc brakes to have the fluid level fall slightly as the pads wear, but cars with drum brakes on all four wheels should not show any drop in fluid level.

CHASSIS & BODY

All suspension points should be lubricated and checked for damage and wear every six months or 12,000 miles. If you have a grease gun, you can do this yourself. If the car is equipped with ball joints, make sure they have grease fittings. If not, you can purchase these at any parts store, thread them in and then use a synthetic grease to lube them. If equipped with manual steering, check the box's fluid level every six months.

Also important is to have your wheel bearings checked and repacked with fresh grease at least once a year or every 12,000 miles.

Brakes

Once again, start fresh by having new pads or shoes installed before the car hits the road. Consider switching to *silicone* brake fluid, as it is less prone to brake line corrosion and won't become contaminated if moisture enters the brake system. Have the rotors and drums cut and use semi-metallic pads or linings as they will last longer. Install new brake cylinders (or if the wheel cylinders are date-coded in your concours car, rebuild them), have the calipers rebuilt and use all new brake hardware.

Make sure that the parking brake works and that all brake lines are in good condition. It is hard to say how long your brakes will last from then on, but under normal driving, you can expect to get 30,000 miles. Visually inspect the pads and shoes at least every six months.

Body Lubrication

Use a high-quality, multi-purpose grease or smooth white body type lubricant at least once a year on the hood hinges and latch, fuel filler door, door and trunk hinges and door latches and lock cylinders (use graphite for the lock cylinders). Lubricate the parking brake assembly and other items such as ashtray slides and concealed headlight doors, if so equipped.

STORAGE

Since most collector cars are spared the abuse of winter driving, the question of proper storage always comes up. As a general rule, it is much better to drive your car occasionally rather than to put it away in long-term storage since all of the fluids circulate and the moisture that accumulates in the engine is burned off. Oils, fluids and gasoline all deteriorate in time, breaking down and creating sludge and varnish. However, in areas where winters are harsh, cars are often put away until spring. What constitutes short-term vs. long-term storage? Six months or less is considered short-term while anything longer is long-term and requires additional steps.

The Garage—The ideal place to store a vehicle is in a well-lit, heated garage that has a wooden floor. A wooden floor absorbs moisture—thereby reducing the possi-

Suspension and steering pickup points need to be lubricated, generally at the same time you change the oil. Photo by Michael Lutfy.

bility of rust formation. Heat does the same thing but its benefits are more readily apparent in the colder, damp months. Heat dissipates moisture and dries the air out. However, most garages have cement floors which absorb moisture but also release it rather quickly. To combat this, plastic sheathing can be placed on the floor and then covered with plywood. The plastic acts as a moisture barrier and the wood absorbs any moisture that gets past the plastic. Bags of silica gel placed in the garage also absorb moisture.

Battery—Some owners remove the battery from the car, while others just remove the positive cable. Leaving the battery in the car could result in corrosion from the battery eating away at the supporting box or tray. Also, an electrical component may fail or a wire could short (even without the key in the ignition), causing a major short-circuit and subsequent fire. If the battery is

Brakes should be checked every 30,000 miles or so, but visually check the pads and shoes every six months . Rotors and drums need to be turned (machined) when you replace pads and shoes. A brake job like this is generally within the realm of most amateur mechanics. You can remove the drums and rotors your-self and have the machining done at a parts shop that offers the service for far less than what a garage will charge to do it for you. It's possible to save hun-dreds of dollars if you do it yourself. Photo by Michael Lutfy.

removed, do not place it directly on a cement floor as the battery will quickly discharge. Instead, place it on a thick piece of wood.

Blocks—One of the big questions regarding storage is whether to put the car on blocks and if so, where to place the blocks—under the frame or the suspension. The best way is to jack the car up using a quality floor jack and place quality jackstands under the front and rear suspension points. Remove the tires and stack them in a corner, placing cardboard between each tire and then covering the tires to avoid fading.

Other Details—Place a tray or several sheets of corrugated cardboard under the oil pan to catch any oil that might leak; you can also put newspapers underneath the engine compartment and transmission to help absorb and pinpoint any possible leaks. Any time a car is placed in storage, even short-term, clean all the windows inside and out, and empty and clean all the ashtrays. Don't put any additional protectant on weatherstripping or in the interior as the moisture in the protectant will attract mold and mildew. Place a handful of mothballs in a tin pie plate and set one on both the front and rear floors of the interior and put another in the trunk. You may also want to seal the tailpipes to stop rats and mice from taking up winter residence.

Always have a fully charged fire extinguisher handy—this may be an insurance requirement anyway. And if your car is particularly valuable, a security system may also be a requirement. It really doesn't pay to skimp when it comes to fire prevention and security.

Long-Term Storage

In addition to the precautions taken for short-term storage, long-term storage requires additional procedures to perform. The gas tank should be drained and the car should be run until all the gasoline remaining in the fuel lines and carburetor is used.

Remove each spark plug and squirt oil in each cylinder, then reinstall the spark plugs. A lightweight oil or white grease should also be used on all body lubrication points. A car cover should be used and the battery should be removed and stored elsewhere.

Removal From Storage

When it is time to take the car out of long-term storage, make sure the battery is fully charged. It can be taken to a service station, checked out and charged or, if you have a trickle charger, put it on the night before it's to be installed.

Check all fluid levels and tire pressure. You may also want to squirt some oil in each cylinder to prevent a "dry" start. Before you start the car up, change the oil and pour a few gallons of gasoline into the tank. Also pour about half a cup full down the carburetor bores. Disconnect the coil wire to prevent the engine from starting and crank the engine to pump oil up into the lifters and valvetrain. Now reconnect the coil wire and start the engine. When it starts, don't rev the engine until it is fully warmed up. Check the fuel pressure gauge or lamp, then look for any leaks in the engine compartment and also check to see that everything works—wipers, lights and any power accessories.

Drive the car slowly and pump the brakes—they may grab initially. Finally, after the drive, check again for any fluid leaks in the engine compartment and look under the car for any transmission and axle leaks. If there are leaks, this can indicate dried-out gaskets or loose hold-down bolts. Tighten any clamps and hold-down bolts to see if that stops the leaks. If not, you'll probably have to replace the gaskets.

Car Covers

There are many types of covers available to choose from. Even though collector cars aren't driven much, they still need protection from dust and other outside debris, especially when they are in storage.

Car covers are available specifically made for your car or you can save a few dollars by getting a "one size fits

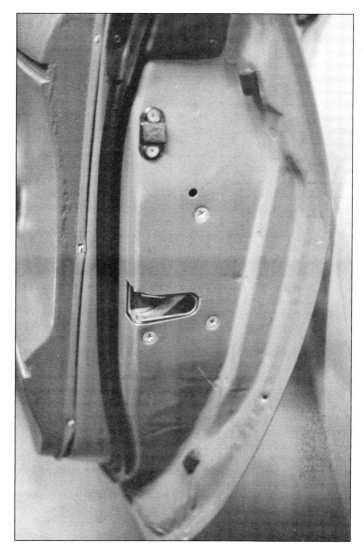

Don't forget to lubricate areas of the car's body, such as hood and trunk lid hinges, door hinges and door jambs where the door secures.

many" that accommodates cars approximately the same size as yours. The most important consideration when purchasing a cover is selecting the right kind of fabric for your specific storage application.

Types of Fabrics—*Cotton flannel* fabrics breathe, allowing air to circulate through them. They are soft and easy on the car's paint and wax. They have no fluid resistance so they should only be used in the dry environment of a garage.

Cotton/polyester fabrics have poor fluid resistance and they trap heat and moisture. Their stiffness can harm your paint and remove wax and they can also fade. When they are treated with a chemical repellent, they lose their ability to breathe. *Nylon* fabrics have the same deficiencies as cotton/polyester.

Long- or short-term, storing your collector car properly requires that you follow some basic procedures. Of great importance is the garage. It should be heated and preferably have a wooden floor which absorbs moisture much more so than cement.

Plastic films should be avoided because they don't breathe, they trap heat and moisture, their stiffness can damage paint, they shrink in the cold and stretch in the heat, and they provide only minimal hail and nick protection. *Vinyl* films should be avoided for the same reasons.

Composite covers made from several layers of material combine the best of each type. For example, covers made from Kimberly/Clark's *Evolution 3* fabric are made in four layers which allow the cover to breathe, repel fluids and provide protection against hail and nicks. Another benefit is that an *Evolution 3* cover will not rot or mildew if folded and stored while it is wet.

If you only plan to use a cover in the garage, then a simple cotton cover is sufficient. If the car is kept outside or if it will be trailered, than the *Evolution 3* fabric will provide the best of all worlds to keep the car's finish clean, dry and scratch-free.

Be sure to coat the tires with a rubber protectorant, such as those available from Eagle One or Meguiar's, prior to long-term storage. Check tire pressures periodically and keep them correct. This is especially important before you drive the car after it has been stored a long time.

Plastic covers should be avoided because they don't breathe, trapping heat and moisture. Their stiffness will also scratch the paint. These cars are being prepped for painting, which is why they are covered with plastic.

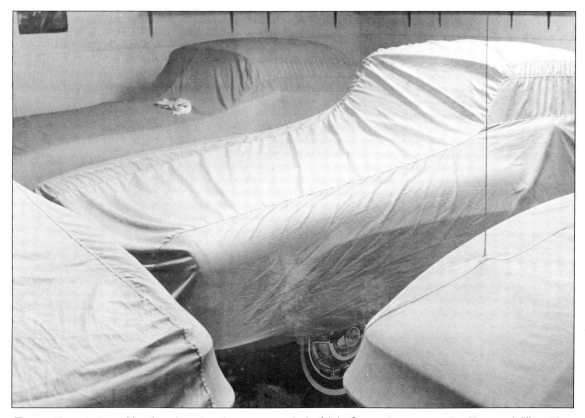

The most important consideration when choosing a car cover is the fabric. Composite covers made with several different layers of breathing and absorbing materials are the best.

7

CAR SHOWS

Car shows vary in size, ranging from small ones like this gathering of Boss 429 Mustangs at a California drive-in to national events that draw thousands of show cars. Photo by Michael Lutfy.

Taking a walk through a field of restored collector cars is like taking a stroll through history, as seen through the eyes of the automobile. Car shows are a gathering of the faithful, where restorers, owners and spectators come together to recall the memories that cars seem to unlock in all of us. Each generation has its favorites, and it's not unusual to see several eras of automotive history displayed on the car show field.

Now, after all of the time, money and work you've invested in your collectible, you finally have a chance to enjoy it and display it proudly in front of colleagues, friends and others who will appreciate your work as much as you do. It's time to enter a car show.

TYPES OF CAR SHOWS

There are several different types of car shows. Some are dedicated to the faithful restoration, others are more liberal in their structure and rules. Some are limited to very specific makes (and sometimes a specific year of a specific make) while others are wide open to any motorized contraption.

Concours

For the correctly restored or pristine original car, a *concours* show is a showcase of ultimate restoration skill and preservation. Generally, marque clubs will conduct a concours show as part of their annual national event. Some clubs hold concours events along with their regular shows because only a small percentage of cars can really qualify for such a demanding event and survive the intense scrutiny of expert judges. A true concours car is no longer driven on the road because even minute particles of dirt and dust are enough to lose points.

Concours Scoring—It's hard work to bring a car up to concours level; restorers will "sweat the details" to

103

Concours cars are judged with extreme prejudice. Judges often look for something wrong. They typically start with a score of 100 and subtract points for flaws. Few, if any cars, are awarded 100 points. Photo by Michael Lutfy.

ensure that their car is absolutely in top shape. In most concours shows, a car is judged against a score sheet. The judge begins with 100 points, and if flaws and errors in the restoration or condition of the car are found as he examines it, points are deducted. The criteria to be a concours judge is knowledge; judges have to be extremely competent about the cars they are examining. Their job is to find things wrong, while they insure that everything on the car is correct. After the judge has finished examining the car, he will tabulate all the deductions found and subtract that from the 100 points he started with. While rule structures vary from show to show and club to club, one thing will always hold true: The car that has the least number of points deducted is the first place winner. Perhaps you have heard the expression, "it's a 99-point car." That indicates the vehicle is about as perfect a

restoration as possible. Few, if any, cars are ever awarded 100 points. That's something to remember when shopping around for a collectible. You should be suspicious if the seller claims the car is a "100-point car."

While some of the most famous classic and exotic cars in the world are shown at the annual Pebble Beach *Concours D'Elegance* in California, many marque clubs and particularly the AACA (Antique Automobile Club of America) point-judge in the concours style on more mundane iron from the Forties, Fifties and Sixties. The AACA accepts cars 25 years or older into their organization, and the club has hundreds of chapters across America that host local and regional shows each year. From these local shows, a car that scores high points can move up to national competition at the annual AACA event in Hershey, Pennsylvania.

Single Marque Shows

By far, what you'll find are shows held by the various marque clubs. Local chapters will hold their own one-day shows once or twice a year while the national club will have a much larger event. For example, the *Shelby American Automobile Club* (SAAC) has a four-day convention each year at a different location, alternating between the east coast, Midwest and west coast in order to give all club members from each area a chance to participate without having to travel very far. Each convention is almost always held near a race track so members can "parade" their cars around.

Because national events are held over a longer period of time, there's more to do than just showing your car. Seminars are often held, with expert club members sharing their knowledge about a particular facet of the car with other members. Many members are all too glad to offer restoration advice, as well as mistakes to avoid. Very often, guest speakers, sometimes from the manufacturers, describe how the cars were built or what the deciding factors were that led to their production. Some events include cruises and, if the event is held at or near a race track, you'll find the cars racing or taking parade laps. And of course, there are the shows. You'll see concours type shows but there will also be more relaxed shows where there is no intensive judging. Some clubs won't bother with any sort of judging; here the emphasis is on enjoying the cars in a more relaxed atmosphere.

Some shows are limited to a single marque. This is a local Corvette show held across the street from Disneyland in Anaheim, California. Nearly 300 Corvettes arrived to be judged. The show featured judging, a parts swap meet, membership drives, technical seminars, and an auction. Photo by Michael Lutfy.

General Interest Shows

Besides the marque club shows, you'll find many shows with several different local or regional clubs participating. These are interesting because you'll see a greater variety of cars from different manufacturers. This can be just as rewarding for both the participant and the spectator. You'll find that the judging in such shows is not as exacting as the typical concours event. In many of these shows, judging is done by "popular vote." Each of the show participants are given a judging sheet to mark their selections for first through third place in each class.

Usually with popular vote shows, craftsmanship can take a back seat to flashy paint. A well-restored four-door sedan can easily lose to a lesser-done red convertible because the rag top has a broader appeal to the general public. Its flashiness will often overlook its flaws.

ISCA—Some of the most popular indoor "World of Wheels" shows are conducted by the ISCA (International Show Car Association, 32285 Mally Drive, Madison Heights, MI 48071). The ISCA holds shows throughout the year at indoor locations in major cities throughout the U.S., with the emphasis on custom and modified cars.

105

Some of the larger national clubs will hold a convention for all members, which can include some track time at a racing facility. Check your insurance policy before you blast out onto the track, however. Photo by Michael Lutfy.

That's not to say you won't see plenty of original, stock, restored collector cars—you will. But ISCA has many classes, unlike other types of shows, that allow wild, modified cars with crazy paint schemes and lots of chrome to compete.

HOW TO SHOW YOUR CAR

Whether you've decided to show your car for competition or you just want to share in the fun with other hobbyists, you'll need to prepare not only the car but two boxes—one for the road and one for the show—before you journey to the show field.

Road Box—The road box should contain parts such as, fan belts, radiator hoses, radiator cap, spark plugs and ignition parts and other minor components that might fail on the way to or at the show. If the trip will be farther from home, a carburetor kit, fuel pump and other hardware might also be packed. A road box should also contain oil, fluids for power steering and brakes, transmis-

sion fluid, a gallon jug of water, anti-freeze, duct tape, safety wire, plenty of rags, PVC tape and a flashlight. Along with the road box, a tool box with a full assortment of wrenches, screwdrivers, sockets, ratchets and extensions, pliers and other tools should be packed.

Show Box—Once you get to the show, you'll need to field-detail the car to freshen it up for judging, especially if you're going to be there for several days. This show box should contain a spray bottle filled with water, a small pail, cotton towels, paper towels, window cleaner, protectorant, sponges, wax, a portable vacuum that plugs into the cigarette lighter or powered by batteries (a whisk broom is fine for home use, but not for car shows because cleanliness is too important), a detail or toothbrush, a small bottle of black paint and exterior paint for touching up rock chips and a magic marker for filling out the show window card. Meguiar's *Quik Detailer* is an excellent, mild, waterless car wash that will remove surface dust without damaging your waxed surface. It is designed for light cleaning at shows.

General interest shows usually have classes for all makes and models. However, competition may not be as keen, so a first place in class at a general interest show may not be the same as one at a single marque show. However, it's still a good opportunity to display your car and talk with people who share your appreciation for it. Photo by Michael Lutfy.

If you will be displaying the car with the trunk open, these boxes can easily be placed under the rear of the car so they are out of the way. Don't forget to take a few folding lawn chairs, a cooler and some snacks.

Registration

If you've preregistered for the show, a packet will be waiting for you when you arrive. If you haven't already done so, you can register when you get there in most cases. Inside the packet will be information for show participants, a dash plaque, a judging sheet and possibly items like coupons, magazine subscriptions and other goodies.

The show officials will place you in the proper class, and once you are parked, you can unload and begin cleaning up the car. If you are displaying the engine, open the

hood and let the engine cool while you wipe down the interior, exterior, window glass and tires. Once the engine compartment is cool, any touch-up or clean-up can then be done. If necessary, use the touch-up paint to repair any chips in the exterior paint, engine compartment or undercarriage. Remember, you should do all major detailing well in advance of the show (see chapter 5). You don't want to arrive at a car show and spend the entire weekend detailing it. Furthermore, a hasty detailing job won't score any points with the judges.

Judging

Once the car is clean, you can sit back and enjoy the show and talk shop with your fellow members. If it's a judged show, make sure you're with the car when the judges come by to answer any questions they may have.

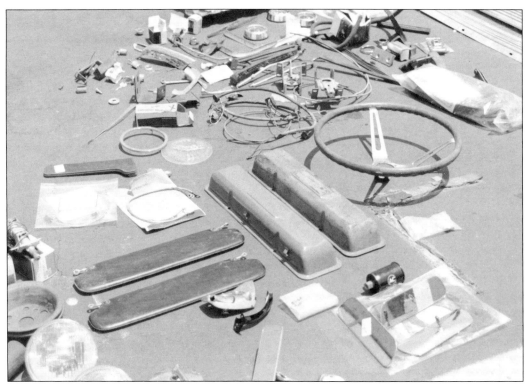

Car shows often have parts for sale, ranging from shiny new reproduction parts to original parts from private parties. Photos by Michael Lutfy.

Give serious thought to how you plan to display your car at the show. This rare Z06 Corvette had an attractive board display listing its fabled history to complement it. Photo by Michael Lutfy.

Well-organized shows may feature technical seminars, where experts on a specific make of car share restoration tips, numbers and data that can help you with your project. Here, famed Corvette historian and restoration expert Noland Adams addresses a group of Corvette enthusiasts. Photo by Michael Lutfy.

Don't try to strike up a conversation with the judge or point out special options and never look over his shoulder as he examines your car. If you are unsure of what is required, contact the show officials beforehand for any show guidelines that may be available.

TRAILERS

Many collector car owners transport their cars on trailers. It's impossible to drive a restored car to a show, enter it in concours competition and expect to place. These cars require a trailer, and for those who can afford it, an enclosed trailer is the best form of transport. It protects the car from rain, dirt and road grime that can ruin the appearance of a concours car, even one that's transported on an open trailer.

Many trailer companies advertise in *Hemmings* with a variety of prices to fit almost every budget. You really don't need a trailer if your car is a fun driver that you enter in local popular vote shows. But, if your collectible is worth the investment, a trailer isn't a luxury, it's a necessity.

It's a good idea to prepare a "show box," which should include supplies to field-detail your car throughout the show. Photo by Michael Lutfy.

One of the nice things about car shows, is that they are an activity the whole family can enjoy. Photo by Michael Lutfy.

APPENDICES

INSURANCE COMPANIES

American Collectors Insurance
P.O. Box 8343
Cherry Hills, NJ 08034
609-779-7212
800-257-5758

Condon & Skelly
121 E. Kings Highway
Maple Shade, NJ 08052
800-257-9496
800-624-4688
609-234-3434

J.C. Taylor Inc.
320 S. 69th Street
Upper Darby, PA 19082
800-345-8290
215-853-1300

The Grundy Agency
P.O. Box 68
Glenside, PA 19038
800-338-4005
215-887-8100

Sneed, Robinson & Gerber, Inc.
6645 Stage Road,
Memphis, TN 38184
901-372-4580

APPRAISERS

Robert DeMars, Ltd.
989 40th Street
North Oakland, CA 94603
415-655-6123

Ted Handler
2028 Cotner Ave.,
Los Angeles, CA 90025
213-479-1197

Lou Trepanier
250 Highland Street
Taunton, MA 02780
508-823-6512

Cy Kay
1160 Waukegan Road
Glenview, IL 60025
312-724-3100

James T. Sandoro
24 Myrtle Ave.,
Buffalo, NY 14204
716-855-1931

James Martin
43 Bowdoin Street
Newton-Highland, MA 02161
617-332-9069

Suncoast Appraisals
9812 105th Circle N.
Largo, FL 34643
813-393-9983

TITLE BUREAUS

Alabama	205-271-3250	Montana	406-846-1424
Alaska	907-269-5551	Nebraska	402-471-3910
Arizona	602-255-7425	Nevada	702-885-5505
Arkansas	501-371-2824	New Hampshire	603-271-3111
California	916-732-7243	New Jersey	609-588-3649
Connecticut	203-566-4410	New Mexico	505-827-7581
Delaware	302-736-4468	New York	518-449-3419
Wash. D.C.	202-727-6680	North Carolina	919-733-3025
Florida	904-488-3881	North Dakota	701-224-2725
Georgia	404-656-4100	Ohio	614-752-7671
Hawaii	808-942-3745	Oklahoma	405-521-3217
Idaho	208-377-6520	Oregon	503-371-2200
Illinois	217-782-9787	Pennsylvania	717-787-3130
Indiana	317-232-2861	Rhode Island	401-277-3100
Iowa	515-281-5277	South Carolina	803-251-2960
Kansas	913-296-3621	South Dakota	605-773-3541
Kentucky	502-564-2737	Tennessee	615-741-2477
Louisiana	504-925-6146	Texas	512-465-7611
Maine	207-289-3071	Utah	801-533-5311
Maryland	301-787-2970	Vermont	802-828-2000
Massachussets	617-727-8500	Virginia	804-257-0523
Michigan	517-322-1624	Washington	206-753-6946
Minnesota	612-296-2977	West Virginia	304-348-3910
Mississippi	601-359-1125	Wisconsin	608-266-1466
		Wyoming	307-638-4307

CAR CLUBS

Abarth

The Abarth Register, USA
1298 Birch St.
Uniondale, L.I., NY 11553
Ph. # 516-481-2092

Alfa Romeo

Alfa Romeo Owners Club
2468 Gum Tree Lane
Fallbrook, CA 92028
Ph. # 619-728-4875

Allard

Allard Owners Club
1 Dalmeny Ave., Tufnell Park
London, England N.7.OLD
Ph. # 071-607-3589

Alvis

Alvis Owners Club
Hill House Farm, Rushock
Near Droitwich
Worcestershire, England
Ph. Chaddesley Corbett 309(056283)

American Motors

AMC Rambler Club (AMCRC, Inc.)
2645 Ashton Rd.
Cleveland Heights, OH 44118
Ph. # 216-371-5946

AMC World Clubs (The Classic AMX Club,
Int. and American Motorsport, Int.)
c/o Linda Mitchell
7963 Depew St.
Arvada, CO 80003-2527
Ph. # 303-428-8760

American Motors Owners Assn.
517 New Hampshire
Portage, MI 49081
Ph. # 616-342-9397

Classic AMX Club Int.
See AMC World Clubs

Marlin Owners Club
RD 5, Box 187
Towerville, PA 19320
Ph. # 215-383-4664

National American Motors Drivers Assn
P.O. Box 987
Twin Lakes, WI 53181
Ph. # 708-599-1255

Total Performance AMC Club
Box 29
Avon Park, FL 33825

Amilcar

Amilcar Register
c/o Ron King
The Apple House, Wildmoor Lane
Sherfield-on-Lodden
Basingstoke, Hampshire, England

Armstrong Siddeley

Armstrong Siddeley Owners Club Limited
Peter Sheppard
57 Barberry Close
Birmingham, B30iTB England

Arnolt-Bristol

Arnolt-Bristol Registry
P.O. Box 60
Brooklandville, MD 21022
Ph. # 301-484-1834

Aston Martin

Aston Martin Owners Club
195 Mount Paran Rd., N.W.
Atlanta, GA 30327
Ph. # 404-436-5314

Auburn-Cord-Duesenberg

Auburn-Cord-Duesenberg Club
Matthew L. Bogart
18 Poplar Road
Ringoes, NJ 08551
Ph. # 908-782-2806

Austin/Bantam

American Austin/Bantam Club
Rt. 1, Box 137
Willshire, OH 45898
Ph. # 419-495-2569

Austin Healey

Austin Healey Association of Southern California
22692 Granite Way
Laguna Hills, CA 92653
Ph. # 714-770-3233

Austin Healey Club of America
603 E. Euclid
Arlington Heights, IL 60004
Ph. # 708-255-4069

Austin Healey Club, Pacific Centre
P.O. Box 6197CP
San Jose, CA 95150
Ph. # 408-867-6201

Austin Healey Sports & Touring Club
P.O. Box 3539
York, PA 17402
Ph. # 717-755-5321

Avanti

Avanti Owners Association Int.
P.O. Box 28788
Dallas, TX 75228-0788
Ph. # 1-800-527-3452

Total Performance Avanti
Dick Datson, Editor
P.O. Box 632
Bradenton, FL 34206

Bentley

Bentley Drivers Club
Dr. Cyril A. Conrad
2139 Torrey Pines Rd.
La Jolla, CA 92037
Ph. # 619-454-1513

Bentley Drivers Club Ltd.
16 Chearsley Rd.
Long Crendon, Aylesbury
Bucks, England HP18 9AW
Ph. # 0844-208233

Berkeley

Berkeley Exchange
46B Elm St.
North Andover, MA 01845
Ph. # 508-587-3421

BMW

BMW Automobile Club of America
P.O. Box 401
Hollywood, CA 90078
Ph. # 818-968-7755

BMW Car Club of America, Inc.
345 Harvard St.
Cambridge, MA 02138
Ph. # 617-492-2500

BMW Car Club of Canada
P.O. Box 232, Station "K"
Toronto, Ontario, Canada M4P 2G5
Ph. # 416-231-3949

BMW 507 Club USA
Hilltown Pike
Hilltown, PA 18927
Ph. # 215-822-8587

BMW Vintage Club of America, Inc.
12661 Kelley Sands Way, #125
Ft. Myers, FL 33908
Ph. # 813-466-5600, FAX 813-466 9563

Vintage BMW Motorcycle Owners, Ltd.
P.O. Box 67
Exeter, NH 03833
Ph. # 603-772-9799

Borgward

Borgward Owners' Club
77 New Hampshire Ave.
Bay Shore, L.I., NY 11706
Ph. # 516-BR-3-0458

West Coast Borgward Owner's Club
644 N. Santa Cruz Ave., Ste. 12-144
Los Gatos, CA 95030
Ph. # 408-395-4971

Bricklin

Bricklin International
5809 Sable Dr.
Alexandria, VA 22303
Ph. # 703-960-2366

Bristol

Bristol Owners' Club
P.O. Box 60
Brooklandville, MD 21022
Ph. # 301-484-1834

Bugatti

American Bugatti Club
400 Buckboard Lane, Persimmon Hill
Ojai, CA 93023

Buick

Buick Car Club of Australia
P.O. Box 177
Richmond, Victoria, Australia   3121

Buick Club of America
P.O. Box 898
Garden Grove, CA 92642

Buick Compact Club, Inc
Rt. 1, Box 39B
Marion, TX 78124
Ph. # 512-625-5914

Buick GS Club of America
1213 Gornto Rd.
Valdosta, GA 31602
Ph. # 912-244-0577

McLaughlin Buick Club of Canada
202 Osborne Rd. E, North Vancouver
BC, Canada V7N lMl
Ph. # 604-324-1273

Buick Skylark Club
P.O. Box 1281
Frederick, MD 21701
Ph. # 413-967-6684

Riviera Owners Assn
P.O. Box 26344
Lakewood, CO 80226
Ph. # 303-987-3712

1932 Buick Registry
3000 Warren Rd.
Indiana, PA 15701
Ph. # 412-463-3372

1937-1938 Buick Club
842 Mission Hills Lane
Worthington, OH 43235
Ph. # 614-687-3041

Cadillac

Cadillac Convertible Owners of America
P.O. Box 269
Ossing, NY 10562

Cadillac LaSalle Club, Inc.
3083 Howard Road
Petoskey, MI 49770
Ph. # 616-347-461

Checker

Checker Car Club of America
469 Tremaine Ave.
Kenmore, NY 14217
Ph.# 716-877-3358

Cartercar Registry
Dick Longcoy
2060 Bethel Road
Landsdale, PA 19446
Ph. # 215-584-4292

Chevrolet

Chevy COPO Connection
P.O. Box 1036
Lombard, IL 60148
Ph. # 708-620-1299

Classic Chevy Club International
P.O. Box 607188
Orlando, FL 32860
Ph.# 407-299-1957

Cosworth Vega Owner's Association
P.O. Box 1783
Bloomington, IN 47402
Ph. # 812-339-0838

Fifty 5-6-7 Club
2021 Wiggins Ave.
Saskatoon
Saskatchewan, Canada S7J lW2
Ph.# 306-343-0567

International Camaro Club, Inc.
2001 Pittston Ave.
Scranton, PA 18505
Ph. # 717-347-5839

Jersey Late Greats, Inc.
P.O. Box 1294
Hightstown, NJ 08520
Ph.# 609-448-0526

Late Great Chevrolet Association
P.O. Box 607824
Orlando, FL 32860
Ph. # 407-886-i963

Long Island Chevy Owners Assoc.
Peter J. Hilcreth
Box 83
Port Jefferson Sta., NY 11776
Ph.# 516-928-5907

Mid-Atlantic Nomad Association
526 East Main St.
Bath, PA 18014
Ph. # 215-837-9669

National Chevelle Owners Association
7343-J West Friendly Ave.
Greensboro, NC 27410
Ph. # 919-854-8935

National Impala Association
P.O. Box 968
Spearfish, SD 57783
Ph. # 605-642-5864

National Monte Carlo Owners Assn., Inc.
P.O. Box 187
Independence, KY. 4105
Ph. # 606-491-2378

National Nomad Club
4691 S. Mariposa Dr.
Englewood, CO 80110
Ph. # 303-761-1964

National Nostalgic Nova
P.O. Box 2344
York, PA 17405
Ph. # 717-252-4192

The 1965-66 Full Size Chevrolet Club
Box 453
Wall Lake, IA 51466
Ph. # 712-664-2427

Tri-Chevy Association
Box 172RB
Elwood, IL 60421
Ph. # 815-478-3633

United States Camaro Club
P.O. Box 608167
Orlando, FL 32860

Vintage Chevrolet Club of America
P.O. Box 5387
Orange, CA 92667

Corvair

Corvair Society of America
P.O. Box 550
Midlothian, IL 60445
Ph. # 312-339-6241

Long Island Chevy Owners Assoc.
Box 83
Port Jefferson Sta., NY 11776
Ph. # 516-928-5907

Corvette

Cascade Corvette Club
P.O. Box 363
Eugene, OR 97440
Ph. # 503-683-2538 or 503-689-1623

Corvettes Unlimited
1120 Fairmont Ave.
Vineland, NJ 08360

National Corvette Owners' Association
900 S. Washington St
Falls Church, VA 22046
Ph. # 703-533-7222

National Corvette Restorers Society
6291 Day Rd.
Cincinnati, OH 45252

National Council of Corvette Clubs, Inc.
P.O. Box 813
Adams Basin, NY
Ph. # 1-800-245-VETT

Western States Corvette Council
2321 Falling Water Court
Santa Clara, CA 95054
Ph. # 408-988-1628

Chrysler (Mopar)

Airflow Club of America
796 Santree Circle
Las Vegas, NV 89110
Ph. # 702-438-4362

California Chrysler Products Club
P.O. Box 2660
Castro Valley, CA 94546
Ph. # 415-889-0533

Challenger 'Cuda Owners Association
R.R. 3
Lachute
Quebec, Canada J8H 3W7
Ph. # 514-562-4426

Chrysler Performance Parts Association
P.O. Box 121O
Azusa, CA 91702
Ph. # 818-303-6220

Chrysler 300 Club, Inc.
P.O. Box 274
Bloomington, IL 61702-0274
Ph. # 309-828-0300

Chrysler 300 Club International, Inc.
19 Donegal Court
Ann Arbor, MI 48104
Ph. # 313-971-3254

Chrysler Town & Country Owners Registry
406 W. 34th
Kansas City, MO 64111
Ph. # 816-931-3341

Daytona-Superbird Auto Club
13717P W. Green Meadow Dr.
New Berlin, WI 53151
Ph. # 414-786-8413

DeSoto Club of America
105 E. 96
Kansas City, MO 64114
Ph. # 816-421-6006

D.A.R.T.S.
P.O. Box 9
Wethersfield, CT 06129-0009
Ph. # 203-296-9008

Dodge Brothers Club
4 Willow St.
Milford, N.H 03055
Ph. # 603-673-6340

1967 & 1968 Dart GTS Registry
Alan Miller
4784 Pioneer Drive
Cedar City, UT 84720

The Dodge Charger Registry
109 Carver Place
Grafton, VA 23692
Ph. # 804-898-1214

1955-56 Dodge La Femme Registry
3752 Third Avenue
San Diego, CA 92103-4112
Ph. # 619-295-2922

Imperial Owners Club, International
P.O. Box 991
Scranton, PA 18503-0991

Low Country Mopars
P.O. Box 60934
North Charleston, SC 29419
Ph. # 803-873-4239

Mopar Muscle Club International
879 Summerlea Ave.
Washington, PA 15301
Ph. # 412-225-5790

Mopar Scat Pack Club
P.O. Box 2303
Dearborn, MI 48123
Ph. # 313-563-5974

National Chrysler Products Club
790 Marigold Ave.
Southampton, PA 18966

National DeSoto Club, Inc.
412 Cumnock Road
Inverness, IL 60067

National Hemi Owners Association
4694 S. Ouray Way
Aurora, CO 80015
Ph. # 303-693-7426

OH Chrysler Touring Club
5198 Harmony Lane
Willoughby, OH 44094
Ph. # 216-942-5506

Northern California Chrysler Products Club
P.O. Box 2660
Castro Valley, CA 94546
Ph. # 415-886-0931

Plymouth Barracuda/Cuda Owners Club
4825 Indian Trail Rd.
Northampton, PA 18067
Ph. # 215-261-2353

Plymouth Cylinder Owners Club, Inc.
Box 416
Cavalier, ND 58220
Ph. # 701-549-3746

The Rapid Transit System
8827 Strathmoor
Detroit, MI 48228
Ph. # 313-838-8030

Slant 6 Club of America
P.O. Box 4414
Salem, OR 97302, SASE please
Ph. # 503-581-2230

Winged Warriors
216-12th St.
Boone, IA 50036
Ph. # 515-432-3001

WPC (Walter P. Chrysler) Club, Inc.
P.O. Box 3504
Kalamazoo, MI 49003-3504

Citroen

Citroen Car Club, Inc.
Box 743
Hollywood, CA 90028
Ph. # 213-255-8691

Crosley

Crosley Automobile Club, Inc.
217 North Gilbert
IA City, IA 52240

Daimler

Daimler & Lanchester Owners' Club of North America
78 William St.
Streetsville
Ontario, Canada L5M lJ3
Ph. # 416-826-8833

Daimler & Lanchester Owners' Club
The Manor House, Abergavenny
Gwent, U.K. NP7 7PG
Ph. # 0873 890704

Datsun/Nissan

Group Z Sports Car Club
P.O. Box 10497
Santa Ana, CA 92711
Ph. # 213-493-3430

Datsun Roadster Assoc.
808 Place Portal Dr.
#AA67
Blaine, WA 98230

Datsun Roadster Owners Club
11337 Cherrylee Dr.
El Monte, CA 91732
Ph. # 312-459-0341

Windy City Z Club
P.O. Box 6009
Evanston, IL 60204-6009
Ph. # 312-459-0341

Davis

Davis 3-Wheel Club of America
Route 2
Argyle, WI 53504
Ph. # 805-395-4523 or 805-871-2548

DeLorean

DeLorean Club International
P.O. Box 23040
Seattle, WA 98102

DeLorean Owners Association
879 Randolph Rd.
Santa Barbara, CA 93111
Ph. # 805-964-5296

Denzel

Denzel Club of America
310 San Vincente
Salinas, CA 93901-4993

DeVaux

DeVaux Registry
240 Greenridge
Grand Rapids, MI 49504
Ph. # 616-784-6640

Durant

Durant Family Registry
2700 Timber Lane
Green Bay, WI 54303-5899
Ph. # 414-499-8797

Edsel

Edsel Owners Club, Inc.
3317 Huguenot Rd.
Richmond, VA 23235
Ph. # 804-272-4987

Edsel Restorers Group
30715 Nine Mile Rd.
Farmington Hills, MI 48024

International Edsel Club
P.O. Box 371
Sully, IA 50251
Ph. # 515-594-4284

Wisconsin Edsel Club
1729 South 24 St.
Milwaukee, WI 53204
Ph. # 414-384-9358

Elva

Elva Owners Club
Maple Tree Lodge, The Hawthornes
Smock Alley, West Chiltington
West Sussex, England RH202QH
Ph. # 0798-812905 FAX: 0903-823710

Ferrari

Ferrari Owners Club
1708 Seabright Ave.
Long Beach, CA 90813
Ph. # 213-432-9607

Ferrari Data Bank
Rt. 3, Box 425
Jasper, FL 32052
Ph. # 904-792-2480

Fiat

Fiat Club of America, Inc.
11 Linden Circle
Somerville, MA 02143-0192
Ph. # 617-776-8576

Ford Products

Crown Victoria Association
P.O. Box 6
Bryan, OH 43506
Ph. # 419-636-2475

Early Ford V8 Club
Box 2122
San Leandro, CA 94577
Ph. # 415-656-5726

Fabulous Fifties Ford Club of America, Inc.
Box 286
Riverside, CA 92502
Ph. # 714-682-3874

Fairlane Club of America
11 Lakeview Ave. R.R. 1
East Peoria, IL 61611
Ph. # 309-822-8602

The Falcon Club of America
P.O. Box 113
Jacksonville, AR 72076
Ph. # 501-982-9721

FOMOCO Owners Club
P.O. Box 19665
Denver, CO 80219
Ph. # 303-935-6662

Ford Data Bank
Rt. 3, Box 425
Jasper, FL 32052
Ph. # (904)-792-2480

Ford Falcon Club of Arizona
11634 N. 29th Place
Phoenix, AZ 85028
Ph. # 602-971-8803

Ford Falcon Club of San Diego
P.O. Box 2156
Spring Valley, CA 92077

Ford & Mercury Restorers Club
P.O. Box 2133
Dearborn, MI 48123

Ford Galaxie Club of America
P.O. Box 2206
Bremerton, WA 98310
Ph. # 206-377-4957

Ford MK II Consul, Zephyr, Zodiac Owners Club
170 Conisborough Cres.
Catford S.E.6.2SH England

International 7-Litre Ford Registry
17 Verdun Drive
Akron, OH 44312
Ph. # 216-794-9015

International Ford Retractable Club, Inc.
P.O. Box 92
Jerseyville, IL 62052
Ph. # 618-498-5485

Long Beach Model T Club, Inc.
5102 Monaco Rd.
Long Beach, CA 90808
Ph. # 213-425-4990

Long Island Ford Mercury Club
c/o L . I . F . M . C .
P.O. Box 336
Ronkonkoma, NY 11779

Model A Ford Club of America
250 S. Cypress
La Habra, CA 90631-5586
Ph. # 213-697-2712 or 697-2737

Model A Restorers Club
24822 Michigan
Dearborn, MI 48124
Ph. # 313-278-1455

Model T Club of Kern County
P.O. Box 885
Bakersfield, CA 93302
Ph. # 805-397-4051

Model T Ford Club International
P.O. Box 438315
Chicago, IL 60643-8315

The Model T Ford Club of America
Box 7400
Burbank, CA 91510
Ph. # 818-842-2010

Nifty Fifties Ford Club of Northern OH
P.O. Box 142
Macedonia, OH 44056

Penn-OH "A" Ford Club, Inc.
48 Gibson Ave.
Mansfield, OH 44907
Ph. # 419-526-3782

Performance Ford Club of America
13155 U.S. Rt. 23
Ashville, OH 43103
Ph. # 614-983-2273

The Ranchero Club
1339 Beverly Rd.
Port Vue, PA 15133
Ph. # 412-678-2670

Special Interest Fords of the Fifties Club
23018 Berry Pine Dr.
Spring, TX 77373
Ph. # 713-288-3351

Twister Specialty Registry
7520 N.W. Rochester Rd.
Topeka, KS 66617
Ph. # 913-246-0155

49-50-51 Ford Owners
P.O. Box 30647
Midwest City, OK 73140
Ph. # 405-737-6021

The 1949 to 1959 Ford Products Club
3655 Maize Rd.
Dept. CPA
Columbus, OH 43224
Ph. # 614-263-3673

Franklin

The H.H. Franklin Club
National Headquarters
Cazenovia College
Cazenovia, NY 13035

Glas

Glas Owners Club
1301 6th Avenue North
Seattle, WA 98109
Ph. # 206-283-9010

Graham

Graham Owners Club International
5262 N.W. Westgate Rd.
Silverdale, WA 98383
Ph. # 206-692-2149

Haynes-Apperson

Haynes & Apperson Owners Club
2125 S. Webster St.
Kokomo, IN 46902
Ph. # 317-453-6373

Hillman

Hillman Owners Club
P.O. Box 94B East Molesey
Surrey, England KT8 9EH

Hispano-Suiza

Hispano-Suiza Society
P.O . Box 4258
Hayward, CA 94540

Honda

Honda Car International
P.O. Box 5242
Deptford, NJ 08096

Hudson-Essex-Terraplane

PHudson-Essex-Terraplane Club, Inc.
HET Club
Box 715CC
Milford, IN 46542
Hupmobile

Hupmobile Club, Inc.
P.O. Box AA
Rosemead, CA 91770

Iso/Bizzarrini

Iso & Bizzarrini Owners Club
P.O. Box 717
Menlo Park, CA 94026-0717
Ph. # 415-321-4604 or 415-339-8347

Jaguar

Classic Jaguar Assn.
1754 Hillcrest Ave.
Glendale, CA 91202
Ph. # 818-244-9132

Jaguar Clubs of North America, Inc.
600 Willow Tree Rd.
Leonia, NJ 07605
Ph. # 201-592-5213

Jeep

See Willys-Overland and AMC

Jensen

Association of Jensen Owners
800 Maywood Ave.
Maywood, NJ 07607
Ph. # 201-845-6851

Jordan

The Jordan Register
58 Bradford Blvd.
Colonial Heights
Yonkers, NY 10710-3699
Ph. # 914-337-5624

Jowett

Dansk Jowett Klub
Boserupvej 510
3050 Humlebaek, Denmark

North American Jowett Register
P.O. Box 4131
Burbank, CA 91503
Ph. # 818-842-5798

Kaiser-Frazer

Kaiser Owners Club, Int.
P.O. Box Y
East Stroudsburg, PA 18301
Ph. # 717-424-8616

King Midget

King Midget Registry
50 Oakwood Drive
Ringwood, NJ 07456

Kissel

Kissel Kar Klub
147 N. Rural St.
Hartford, WI 53027-1407
Ph. # 414-673-7999

Kurtis Kraft Register

Kurtis Kraft Register
Drawer 220
Oneonta, NY 13820
Ph. # 607-432-6835

Lagonda

Lagonda Club Spares Scheme
Dormer Cottage, Woodham Park Way
Woodham Weybridge
Surrey KT15 3SD England 09323 46359

The Lagonda Club
3237 Harvey Parkway
Oklahoma City, OK 73118
Ph. # 405-232-3100 (Office) or 405-521-1998 (Home)

Lamborghini

Lamborghini Club of America
4 Sol Brea Way
Orinda, CA 94563
Ph. # 415-254-2107

Lancia

American Lancia Club
2100 E. OH St.
Pittsburgh, PA 15212
Ph. # 412-323-1124

Dansk Lancia Register
Boserupvej 510
3050 Humlebaek, Denmark

Lancia Motor Club Ltd.
26B Mopley Close, Blackfield
Southampton
Hants S04 1YL England
Ph. # 0703 898848

Lincoln

Colorado Continental Convertible Club
683 S. Carr Street
Lakewood, CO 80226
Ph. # 303-986-8402

The Continental Mark II Owners Assn.
26676 Holiday Ranch Rd.
Apple Valley, CA 92307
Ph. # 619-247-4758

Lincoln & Continental Owners Club
P.O. Box 549
Nogales, AZ 85628
Ph. # 602-281-8193

Lincoln Cosmopolitan Owners Registry
P.O. Box 1600
Sutter Creer, CA 95686-1600

Lincoln Owners' Club, Inc.
22 Spring St.
Cary, IL 60013
Ph. # 312-639-7434

Lincoln Zephyr Owner's Club
2107 Steinruck Rd.
Elizabethtown, PA 17022

Road Race Lincoln Register
461 Woodland Drive
Wisconsin Rapids, WI 54494
Ph. # 715-423-9579

Lotus

Club Elite of North America
6238 Ralston Ave.
Richmond, CA 94805
Ph. # 415-232-7764

Golden Gate Lotus Club
P.O. Box 117303
Burlingame, CA 90411
Ph. # 415-348-0309

Lotus, Limited
P.O. Box L
Collese Park, MD 20740

Lotus Seven Club Deutschland
Post Box li 10 14
D-4000 Dusseldorf, West Germany

Marmon

Marmon Club
P.O. Box 8031
Canton, OH 44711
Ph. # 216-454-7070

Maserati

Maserati Club
The Paddock, Old Salisbury Rd.
Abbotts Ann, Andover
Hampshire, England SPll 7NT
Ph. # UK 0264-710312

Mazda

Mazda Club
P.O. Box 11238
Chicago, IL 60611

Mazda RC-7 Club
1774 S. Alvira St.
Los Angeles, CA 90035
Ph. # 213-933-6993

Mercedes-Benz

Gull Wing Group, Int's.
2229 Via Cerritos
Palos Verdes Estates, CA 90274
Ph. # 213-375-8630

International 190 SL Group
190 SL Group
3 Westpark Court
Ferndale, MD 21061

Mercedes-Benz Club of America, Inc.
P.O. Box 9985
Colorado Springs, CO 80932
Ph. # 800-637-2360 (outside Colorado)
719-633-6427 (in Colorado)

Mercer

Mercer Associates
414 Lincoln Ave
Havertown, PA 19083
Ph. # 215-446-0138

Mercury

Mercury Enthusiast Restorer/Custom/Performance
Auto Club (Merc-Pac)
Rt. 4, Box 116
Alexandria, IN 46001-9413
Ph. # 317-724-7601

American Comet Club/Merc-Pac
Rt. 4, Box 116
Alexandria, IN 46001-9413
Ph. # 317-724-7601

Classic Comet Club of America
Rd. 3, Box 3456
Fleetwood, PA 19522

Cougar Club of America
18660 River Cliff Dr.
Fairview Park, OH 44126

Mid-Century Mercury Car Club
1816 E. Elmwood Dr.
Lindenhurst, IL 60046
Ph. # 708-356-2255

United Spoiler of America/Merc-Pac
Rt. 4, Box 116
Alexandria, IN 460Q1-9413
Ph. # 317-724-7601

Cougar Club of Canada
P.O. Box 426, Station A
#17-3605 Portage Ave.
Winnipeg
Manitoba, Canada R3K 2C2

South Central Cougar Club
8622 S, 78th East Ave.
Tulsa, OK 74133
Ph. # 918-250-1842

Metz

Metz Owners Club Library
Seven Lakes, Box 2055
West End, NC 27376
Ph. # 919-673-1607

Metropolitan

Metropolitan Owners' Club
4 Burnham Rd., Dnaphill
Woking
Surrey, England GU21 2AE
Ph. # 04867-4841(within U.K.)

Metropolitan Owners Club of North America, Inc.
5009 Barton Rd.
Madison, WI 53711
Ph. # 608-271-0457

Metropolitan Owners Club of North America
5009 Barton Rd.
Madison, WI 53711

MG

American MGB Assn.
P.O. Box 11401
Chicago, IL 60611
Ph. # 312-843-3897

American MGC Register
27 Pembrook Dr.
Stony Brook, NY 11790
Ph. # 516-751-8107

Bluegrass MG
1400A Browns Lane
Louisville, KY 40207
Ph. # 502-499-7867 or 502-893-8800

California MG "T" Register
4911 Winnetka Ave.
Woodland Hills, CA 91364
Ph. # 818-883-9681

Classic MG Club of Florida
1307 Ridgecrest Rd.
Orlando, FL 32806
Ph. # 305-859-0173

M.G. Car Club
P.O. Box No. 25;
Studley
Warwickshire, B80.7AT, U.K.
Ph. # U.K. (52785) 3666

MG Octagon Car Club
36 Queensville Ave
Starford ST17 4LS, England
Ph. # 0785-51014

Midwest MGA Club
7906 Bradshaw
Lenexa, KS 66215
Ph. # 913-541-1485

New England MG T Register, Ltd.
Drawer 220
Oneonta, NY 13820
Ph. # 607-432-6835

So Cal Association-MG Club
5032 Lenore St.
Torrance, CA 90503
Ph. # 213-540-0668

North American MGA Register
76 Blossom Lane
Mooresville, IN 46158

Vintage M.G. Car Club of Chicago
P.O. Box 160
Franklin Park, IL 60131
Ph. # 312-455-0388

Mini

North American Mini Moke Registry
P.O. Box 9110
South Lake Tahoe, CA 95731
Ph. # 916-577-7895

Mini Registry
876 Turk Hill Road
Fairport, NY 14450
Ph. # 716-388-0088

Mitchell

Mitchell Registry Box 416
Cavalier, ND 58220
or
R.R. 2, Box 73C
Coal Valley, IL 61240
or
12921-74th Place NE
Kirkland, WA 98033

Morgan

Morgan Car Club of Washington, D.C.
616 Gist Ave.
Silver Spring, MD 20910
Ph. # 301-585-0121

Morgan Owners of Philadelphia
P.O. Box 242K
Martins Creek, PA 18063
Ph. # 215-253-5327

Morgan Sports Car Club
Hollands Farm (CP) Coombe Green
Birtsmorton
Malvern, England WR13 6AB

The 3/4 Morgan Group Ltd.
P.O. Box 474
New Paltz, NY 12561
Ph. # 201-984-5431

Morgan Three Wheeler Club (UK)
6614 E. Corrine Drive
Scottsdale, AZ 85254
Ph. # 602-948-2591

Morris

Bullnose Morris Club
P.O. Box 383
Hove
East Sussex, England BN3 4FX

Morris Minor Registry
86 Wayland St.
North Haven, CT 06518
Ph. # 203-248-9255

Morris Register
171 Levita House
Chalton St., London NW1 1HR

Mustang

Mustang and Classic Ford Club of New England
197 Ellis Rd.
No. Attleboro, MA 02760

Mustang Car Club of New England
P.O. Box 1554
Woonsocket, RI 02895
Ph. # 401-737-2681

Mustang Club of America, Inc.
P.O. Box 447
Lithonia, GA 30058-0447
Ph. # 404-482-4822

Mustang Club of Southern California
15168 Ashwood Lane
Chino, CA 91710
Ph. # 714-597-2509

Mustang Owners Club International
2720 Tennesee NE
Albuquerque, NM 87110
Ph. # 505-296-2554

Mustang Owners Club of California
P.O. Box 8261
Van Nuys, CA 91409
Ph. # 818-609-8009

The North Jersey Mustang Club
P.O. Box 212
Northvale, NJ 07647
Ph. # 201-768-2129

National Capital Region Mustang Club
9307 Shouse Dr.
Vienna, VA 22180
Ph. # 703-938-3746

Orange County Mustang Club
15168 Ashwood Lane
Chino, CA 91709
Ph. # 714-597-2509

'70 429 Mustang Registry
6250 Germantown Pk.
Dayton, OH 45418

'68 Mustang GT/CA Special Registry
P.O. Box 2013
El Macero, Ca 95618

Shelby: See separate Shelby classification.

NASH

Little Nash Rambler Club
P.O. Box 1385
Sequim, WA 98382-1385

Nash Car Club of America
R.R. #1, Box 253
Nash Nook
Clinton, IA 52732
Ph. # 319-242-5490

Nash-Healey Car Club
530 Edgewood Ave.
Trafford, PA 15085
Ph. # 412-372-3952

NSU

NSU Enthusiasts USA
11192 Prouty Road
Concord, OH 44077
Ph. # 216-354-4403

Oldsmobile

Curved Dash Oldsmobile Owners Club
7 Kiltie Dr.
New Hope, PA 18938
Ph. # 215-862-2353

Hurst/Olds Club of America
1600 Knight Rd.
Ann Arbor, MI 48103

Mid-Texas Oldsmobile Club
8912 Sharpstone Trail
Austin, TX 78717

National Antique Oldsmobile Club
Box 483
Elmont, NY 11003
Ph. # 516-285-7311

Oldsmobile Club of America
P.O. Box 16216
Lansing, MI 48901

Opel

North American Opel GT Club
2641 Starlite Dr.
Joliet, IL 60433
Ph. # 815-723-4801

Opel Drivers Club of America
P.O. Box 385
Pebble Beach, CA 93953
Ph. # 408-754-6359

Opel Motorsport Club A.G.
14176 Fort Apache Court
Victorville, CA 92392

Opel USA
64 Eaton Rd.
Tolland, CT 06084
Ph. # 203-872-4412

Packard

The Eastern Packard Club, Inc.
99 Quaker Lane
Fairfield, CT 06430
Ph. # 203-259-9371

Packard Data Bank
Rt. 3, Box 425
Jasper, FL 32052
Ph. # 904-792-2480

The Packard Club/Packard Automobile
Classics, Inc.
P.O. Box 2808
Oakland, CA 94618

Packards International Motor Car Club
302 French St.
Santa Ana, CA 92701
Ph. # 714-541-8431

Pantera

Pantera International
5540 Farralone Ave.
Woodland Hills, CA 91367
Ph. # 818-992-1139

Peugeot

Peugeot Owners' Club
5113 Dickson Rd.
Indpls., IN 46226
Ph. # 317-545-2825

Pierce-Arrow

Pierce-Arrow Society, Inc.
135 Edgerton St.
Rochester, NY 14607

Pontiac

GTO Association of America
1634 Briarson Dr.
Saginaw, MI 48603

National Firebird Club
P.O. Box 11238-F
Chicago, IL 60611

Oakland-Pontiac Enthusiast Organization, Inc.
2425 Walnut Rd.
Auburn Hills, MI 48057
Ph. # 313-334-6998

Original GTO Club Int.
P.O. Box 18438
Milwaukee, WI 53218

Pontiac-Oakland Club International, Inc.
P.O. Box 4789
Culver City, CA 90230
Ph. # 818-704-1580

The Judye GTO Int.
114 Prince George Dr.
Hampton, VA 23669
Ph. # 804-838-2059

Trans Am Club U.S.A.
Box 99
Medford, MA 02153

Worldwide Fiero Club
835 E. 23rd Avenue
New Smymabch, FL 32169

Porsche

Porsche 356 Registry
P.O. Box 85018
Ft. Wayne, IN 46885-5018
Ph. # 219-486-4448

Porsch 914 Owners Association
611 South Palm Canyon #7
Suite 165A
Palm Springs, CA 92264

Porsche Owner's Club 19831 Ventura Blvd.
Woodlands Hills, CA 91364
Ph. # 818-712-0106

Powell

Powell Cycle Registry
4588 Pacific Hwy. North
Central Point, OR 97502
Ph. # 503-664-2641

Powell Sport Wagon Registry
Box 27871
Tempe, AZ 85285
Ph. # 602-834-4643

Railton

Railton Owners Club
Fairmiles Barnes Hall Rd.
Burncross
Sheffield, England S30 4RF
Ph. # 0742-468357

Renault

Renault Owners Club of America
1380-156th Ave. NE, #204
Bellevue, WA 98007
Ph. # 206-882-0352

Reo

Reo Club of America
Box 462, RD 1
Cogan Station, PA 17728
Ph. # 717-435-0555

Rickenbacker

Rickenbacker Car Club of America
Star Route, Box 92B
Saranac Lake, NY 12983
Ph. # 518-891-2247

Riley

The Riley Motor Club U.S.A., Inc.
P.O. Box 4162
Anaheim, CA 92803

Rolls-Royce

Phantom III Technical Society
P.O. Box 25
Mechanicsburg, PA 17055
Ph. # 717-697-1950

Rolls-Royce Enthusiasts' Club
R.R. 2, The Hunt House
Paulerspury
Northants, England NN2 7NA
Ph. # 032-733-788

The Rolls-Royce Owners' Club, Inc.
191 Hempt Road
Mechanicsburg, PA 17055
Ph. # 717-697-4671

Saab

New England Sonett Club
P.O. Box 4362
Manchester, NH 03108

Saab Club of North America
2416 London Road - Unit 900
Duluth, MN 55812
Ph. # 218-724-1336

Sabra

Sabra Connection
7040 N. Navajo Ave
Milwaukee, WI 53217
Ph. # 414-352-8408

Saxon

Saxon Registry
5250 N.W. Highland Dr.
Corvallis, OR 97330
Ph. # 503-752-6231

Shelby

Shelby American Automobile Club
P.O. Box 788
Sharon, CT 06069

Shelby Owners of America, Inc.
577 14 St. S.E.
LeMars, IA 51031
Ph. # 712-546-4045

Singer

North American Singer Owners Club
2113 S. Avenida Planeta
Tucson, AZ 85710
Ph. # 602-747-2901

Star of England

Star Starling Stuart & Briton Car Register
9 Compton Dr.
Dudley
West Midlands, England DY2 7ES
Ph. # Dudley 54768

Stevens-Duryea

Stevens-Duryea Associates
Warwick Eastwood
3565 Newhaven Rd.
Pasadena, CA 91107
Ph. # 818-351-8237

Studebaker

Avanti: See Separate Avanti classification.

Antique Studebaker Club, Inc.
P.O. Box 28845
Dallas, TX 75228
Ph. # 214-709-6185

Erskine Register
441 E. St. Clair
Almont, MI 48003
Ph. # 313-798-8600

Total Performance Studebaker Club
Box 29
Avon Park, FL 33825

Studebaker Drivers Club Inc.
P.O. Box 28788
Dallas, TX 75228-0788
Ph. # 800-527-3452, foreign 214-709-6185

Studebaker Drivers Club Inc.
P.O. Box 28788
Dallas, TX 75228-0788
Ph. # 800-527-3452

Stutz

The Stutz Club
7906 S. 10th St.
Kalamazoo, MI 49009
Ph. # 616-375-4844

Subaru

Subaru 360 Drivers' Club 4934 E. Timrod St.
Tucson, AZ 85711
Ph. # 602-326-6402

Sunbeam

California Association of Tiger Owners
5165 Slauson Ave.
Culver City, CA 90230
Ph. # 213-391-8973

Sunbeam Alpine Club/or Rootes
Registry Sunbeam
1752 Oswald Pl.
Santa Clara, CA 95050
Ph. # 408-984-1474

Tigers East/Alpines East
RD. 4, Box 54
Tunkhannock, PA 18657
Ph. # 717-836-4111

Thunderbird

Classic Thunderbird Club Int.
P.O. Box 4148
Santa Fe Springs, CA 90670
Ph. # 213-945-6836

Rocky Mountain Thunderbird Club
15600 W. 1st Dr.
Golden, CO 80401
or
451 E. 58th Ave., Suite 1185
Denver, CO 80216
Ph. # 303-278-9043 or 303-295-2297

Thunderbirds of America
Box 2766
Cedar Rapids, IA 52406
Ph. # 319-364-6859

Vintage Thunderbird Club International
P.O. Box 2250
Dearborn, MI 48123

Triumph

Triumph Register of America
804 North High St.
Lancaster, OH 43130
Ph. # 614-653-1686

Triumph Roadster Club
The Woodlands, Taddington
NR Buxton
Derbyshire SK17 9UD England
Ph. # 0298 85308

Triumph Sports Owners Assn
P.O. Box 36477
Grosse Pointe, MI 48236

Triumph Sports Six Club
121B St. Marus Rd., Market Harborough
Leicestershire, England LE16 7DT
Ph. # (0858) 34424, FAX 0858 31936

Vintage Triumph Register
P.O. Box 36477
Grosse Pointe, MI 48236
Ph. # 201-691-8116

6-Pack Triumph TR-6
11792 Thomas Spring Rd.
Monrovia, MD 21770

Tucker

Tucker Automobile Club of America
311 W. 18th St.
Tifton, GA 31794

TVR

TVR Car Club North America
4450 S. Park Ave., Apt. 1609
Chevy Chase, MD 20815
Ph. # 301-986-8679 (home) or
301-864-4330 (work)

Volkswagen

National Capital Area Volkswagen Club
P.O. Box 235
New Market, MD 21774
Ph. # 301-865-3746

Vintage Volkswagen Club of America
818 Main St.
Portage, PA 15946
Ph. # 814-736-4343

Volvo

Volvo Club of America
31 Pine St.
Peterborough, NH 03458
Ph. # 603-924-6026

Volvo Owners' Club
34 Lyonsgate Drive
Downsview
Ontario, Canada M3H lC8
Ph. # 416-633-6801 (home)
416-447-6465 (office)

Volvo Sports America 1800, Inc.
1203 W. Cheltenham Ave.
Melrose Park, PA 19126
Ph. # 215-635-0117

Washington Volvo Club, Inc.
8608 Saffron Dr.
Lanham, MD 20706
Ph. # 301-552-1696

White

White Owners' Register
1624 Perkins Dr.
Arcadia, CA 91006
Ph. # 818-355-7679

Wills Sainte Claire

The Wills Club
721 Jenkinson
Port Huron, MI 48060
Ph. # 313-987-2425

Willys-Overland

Midstates Jeepster Assn.
12604 Vivian Ct.
Rockton, IL 61072
Ph. # 815-624-2068

West Coast Willys Club
222 S. San Clemente
Ventura, CA 93001

Willys Aero Survival Count, Int.
c/o Rick Kamen
220 North Brighton St.
Burbank, CA 91506
Ph. # 818-843-0677

Willys Club
719 Lehigh St.
Bowmanstown, PA 18030
Ph. # 215-852-3110

Willys-Overland Jeepster Club, Inc.
P.O. Box 12042
El Paso, TX 79913
Ph. # 915-581-2671

Willys-Overland-Knight Registry
11705 Bradley Forest Rd.
Manassas, VA 22111
Ph. # 703-369-6511

HP Automotive Books

HANDBOOK SERIES

Auto Electrical Handbook
Auto Math Handbook
Baja Bugs & Buggies
Brake Handbook
Camaro Restoration Handbook
Clutch & Flywheel Handbook
Metal Fabricator's Handbook
Mustang Restoration Handbook
Off-Roader's Handbook
Paint & Body Handbook
Sheet Metal Handbook
Small Trucks
Street Rodder's Handbook
Turbochargers
Turbo Hydra-Matic 350
Welder's Handbook

CARBURETORS

Holley 4150
Holley Carburetors & Manifolds
Rochester Carburetors
Weber Carburetors

PERFORMANCE SERIES

How to Hot Rod Big-Block Chevys
How to Hot Rod Small-Block Chevys
How to Hot Rod Small-Block Mopar Engines
How to Hot Rod VW Engines
How to Make Your Car Handle
Small-Block Chevy Performance

REBUILD SERIES

How to Rebuild Air-Cooled VW Engines
How to Rebuild Big-Block Chevys
How to Rebuild Big-Block Ford Engines
How to Rebuild Small-Block Chevys
How to Rebuild Small-Block Ford Engines
How to Rebuild Small-Block Mopars
How to Rebuild Your Ford V-8

SPECIAL INTEREST

Auto Repair Shams & Scams
Car Collector's Handbook
Fast Fords
Guide to GM Muscle Cars

Books are available from your local auto store, bookstore or order direct from publisher, Price Stern Sloan
11150 Olympic Boulevard, Sixth Floor, Los Angeles, CA 90064.
Call toll-free: 800/421-0892.